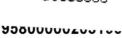

D1588353

Speak

FIND YOUR VOICE, TRUST YOUR GUT, and GET FROM WHERE YOU ARE TO WHERE YOU WANT TO BE

Speak

Tunde
Oyeneyin

with Hilary Liftin

GALLERY BOOKS UK

First published in the United States by Avid Reader Press,
an imprint of Simon & Schuster, Inc., 2022

First published in Great Britain by Gallery Books,
an imprint of Simon & Schuster UK Ltd, 2022

1 3 5 7 9 10 8 6 4 2

Simon & Schuster UK Ltd
1st Floor
222 Gray's Inn Road
London WC1X 8HB

www.simonandschuster.co.uk
www.simonandschuster.com.au
www.simonandschuster.co.in

Simon & Schuster Australia, Sydney
Simon & Schuster India, New Delhi

A CIP catalogue record for this book
is available from the British Library

Hardback ISBN: 978-1-3985-1217-7
eBook ISBN: 978-1-3985-1219-1

Interior design by Lewelin Polanco

Printed in the UK by CPI Group (UK) Ltd, Croydon, CR0 4YY

For my mother and father,
Veronica and Festus Oyeneyin.
Through your lessons, I found my voice.

For my brother Tope Oyeneyin.
Because of you, I speak.

Contents

Contents

Introduction

No matter who we are, no matter where we are, no matter what we are going through or whether we've asked for it, we all have that one moment. A moment when you see clearly how your life might change—the only decision you have to make is if you're going to pay attention to the fact that it's there.

I had one of those moments in 2016, just after I finished the first cycling class I'd ever taken. I was in New York, feeling lost and disconnected, confused about who I was and what I was doing with my life. It was a very uncomfortable place to be, but I didn't know exactly how to shake myself out of it. I left the fitness studio, still feeling that after-workout high; movement had helped. As I made my way home, something made me stop short. Out of nowhere, I threw my face into my hands and let out a loud laugh—not a giggle or a chuckle but a burst of pure, unfiltered joy. After a long period of feeling uncertain about what was to come, I suddenly felt wildly grateful to be alive. Something was happening with my soul and my spirit. I had gone from skipping through the fog of New York City to laughing like a crazy person. Then a rush of energy moved through me. I felt a blue light run from my toes to my fingertips.

For the first time in a while—perhaps the first time ever—I could see it clearly. My future. I would be cycling for the rest of my life. And not only that, but I'd be teaching it to others. On the world's biggest platform. As I had these thoughts, I didn't even really know what they meant. But they were as clear to me as anything had ever been. I was absolutely certain.

By the time I got home, the sensation had faded, but the thoughts stayed in the back of my head. I could have dismissed them and gone on with my regularly scheduled programming, telling myself that things were good enough, or that what I'd experienced on that walk were fantasies, ignoring the feeling deep down that something had to change. I could have stuck with what felt comfortable and familiar and made sense.

But I didn't.

Fast-forward to 2021. I had become one of Peloton's elite instructors, training millions of people across four countries every day from a bike on a podium. It was a dream job. I didn't get there in one day, or even one year. But the moment I had—the *vision* I had—opened a door, and I shoved my foot right into it until, little by little, I squeezed my way in.

I know what you're thinking: *Tunde, easier said than done! Life is hard! There are responsibilities! We can't just drop everything to chase a moment.* And that's true. But I want to challenge that thought for a minute and ask: What if that moment isn't just a moment, but a mindset?

We are often so trapped by our expectations of ourselves and our lives. Life can be complicated, and to protect ourselves, we assume we know what's to come and look for a path that's wide and clear, well-blazed with trail markers so we get it right. But in our quest to make things easier, we often unintentionally impose limits. We fail to notice the side roads, the alternate routes, the opportunities to scramble up a rock face over which we might see a big, open sky. Knowing what's next keeps you knowing only what you know. Embracing uncertainty empowers you to take risks. The beauty of uncertainty, I've found, is infinite possibility.

When I'm teaching a class, I like to say things twice, so riders have a chance to absorb what I'm trying to say—so *I* have a chance to absorb what I'm trying to say.

So, here it is again: *The beauty of uncertainty is infinite possibility.*

I hope that's how you feel opening this book. Maybe you came to it because you've taken my class, maybe your friend gave it to you, maybe you liked the cover. You don't even have to have heard of me before or clicked into a stationary bike to join in. I will do my best to give you a reason to move forward with me, in whatever ways we can. We won't always move forward chronologically, or as things happened in the moment—after all, that's not really how stories work. When we sit down with our friends, we don't fill them in on our lives from beginning to end. We get ahead of ourselves and circle back; echoes of the past inform the future; we wait until we know each other a little better, until the time is just right.

When I teach, I'm always trying to lead riders forward with thoughts and directions I hope will be inspiring. We're on the bike alone, but we ride together. Every day, I see people grow physically, spiritually, emotionally, and mentally by taking that first, hundredth, or thousandth step. That's what I've tried to do here. I've created a path for you with my words, but the journey is your own.

We all have moments like my blue-light vision at least a few times in our lives, even if they don't come in that exact form. You feel like something you didn't even know you were waiting for is right in front of you. And you have to decide how you are going to act. Are you open enough to receive the message? Brave enough to surrender to the mystery of a new direction? Strong enough to pursue your vision, even if it doesn't fall into your lap? Or will you choose to stay comfortable? Those were the questions I asked myself, and listening to how I answered them, listening to my friends, to the voices around me, and the universe at large got me where I am today, realizing that my life's mission is to SPEAK.

SPEAK is about finding my voice, but it is also the movement I've created for others, using five key pillars:

Speak

SURRENDER

POWER

EMPATHY

AUTHENTICITY

KNOWLEDGE

In order to speak, you have to be willing to surrender. You have to know your power. You have to lead with empathy. You have to be authentic, and you have to have the knowledge to back it.

These words shape my philosophy. They keep me strong and vulnerable, caring and tough, curious and ready. They keep me moving forward, on flat ground, up hills, even when it looks and feels like I'm staying in one place. They have carried me through all the stories I will share in this book—times of great sorrow and heartbreak, change, triumph, and joy. They have brought me the best of friendships; they have connected me with people I never thought I'd meet; and they have brought me here, to you. I'm sharing them and the lessons they offer because my greatest dream is that each of us finds love, peace, and acceptance for ourselves, and then brings that love out into the world.

I want this book to help you take notice of where these words, as concepts, have shown up in major moments in your life. On a piece of paper, or in your phone if, like me, you have it attached to your hip, write down these five words and think about your own life.

If you look back, you may find that when you surrendered, it resulted in change. When you led with empathy, you found yourself able to act more freely. Once you're aware of these words, you can tune in to them and give yourself the license to act in that spirit. Recognizing where you are allows you to move more freely into action.

Every day, I see regular people push themselves out of their comfort zones. I see them reach out to each other. I see them connect and grow. And that's because, I believe, in some ways we're all the same. We all feel the same grief, joy, and hope, and we all have the capacity to create change for ourselves and others. Why not the whole world? Why not surrender to the unknown, step into our power, lead with empathy, be true and authentic to ourselves along the way, and use the knowledge that we gain to get us from where we are to where we want to be? How do we SPEAK?

This is how.

Speak

ONE

The Perfect Dress

I'm a fitness instructor at Peloton and a Nike athlete, two of the top platforms for a person with a strong, healthy body, so it might seem obvious for me to lead off with a story about body image, but it's where we all begin. We all have a body. It's the first thing that belongs to us. It's where we live and how we move through the world, and our experience within it guides us into the different paths we take as we grow. When we transform it, it transforms us.

When I was fourteen years old, I was a bridesmaid in my auntie's wedding. I'm first-generation American—my parents emigrated from Nigeria to Houston, Texas, before I was born—and in Nigerian families, we call all our elders "auntie" and "uncle." It's like having many parents. All my warm, chatty, Nigerian aunties talked to me as if I were their child, and my mother treated their children as if they were her own. We were often in each other's houses

Tunde Oyeneyin

for meals. Sometimes my cousins would come over to our house and stay for days.

Being a bridesmaid meant that I needed a new, fancy dress. I was so excited. My mom and I drove to a bridal store in the south part of Houston. My auntie was already there when we arrived.

"This is the dress!" she announced as we walked in. I looked at the store clerk, who was holding up a full-length, cobalt-blue satin dress with a boat neck, capped sleeves, and a pleated skirt. *Oh.* I was full-figured: I had bigger breasts, larger thighs, and was chubby-faced. I wasn't particularly excited about wearing a dress with capped sleeves that would draw attention to my big arms. I had been picturing something that would make me look and feel like a princess. Blue was my favorite color, but in my opinion, it was wasted on this particular dress. The dress was an insult to cobalt. Maybe that's too strong. It was just plain ugly. My auntie was a stylish woman, so I'd expected something a little more exciting, but it was her big day. I would do whatever made her happy.

"Can we see it in a size eighteen, please?" my mom asked the clerk.

The clerk glanced at me, and I saw a flash of doubt pass over her face, but then she smiled and said, "Of course. Let me check on that." Instead of going to the rack, she went to her computer. After a moment, she returned and said, "I'm sorry to say that this dress doesn't come in a size larger than twelve."

I was mortified. It hadn't occurred to me that I might be too big for the dress my auntie had picked.

Speak

The first time I felt self-conscious about my size was in third grade. My friends at school weren't yet at the age where certain questions were considered too personal to ask, so a group of us were standing around in the schoolyard comparing our weights. I was the third to volunteer my weight, and I did so without hesitation: I was 116 pounds. The kids' mouths dropped open. Brian looked at Rachel and said with awe, "Tunde's in the hundreds!"

"Wow, that's a lot!" exclaimed Rachel. Then they continued around the rest of the circle. None of my friends had hit triple digits yet. That hadn't even occurred to me. My auntie had a younger daughter whom she always told, "You need to eat so you can be fat like your cousin Yetunde," but it was more a practical statement than a judgmental one—she just wanted her daughter to have the benefit of my hand-me-downs. I had good clothes and always spent my allowance and birthday money on them. Every Saturday morning, my mother and I went to garage sales together looking for good deals. From the time I was little, I'd treated school as if it were a fashion show and arrived ready to fingerpaint in my Easter Sunday finest. As I got older I wore the cheap version of the trendiest styles.

I had three brothers—Tony and Tosin were older than me, and Tope was younger than me. They were all athletic and very big eaters. We lived off the ninety-nine-cent Whoppers at Burger King, or the McRib at McDonald's when it was in season. A serving size for me was two burgers, and I never thought twice about it. We all ate whatever we wanted. Sometimes my brothers teased me, calling me fat, but my mom was pleased when we ate. Eating was a sign of health and a gesture of respect for the person who had prepared the food. When I complained about my brothers, my mother just said, "If they make fun of you, stand up straight and give it right back to them." So when my brothers called me fat, I popped back at them, "At least I can lose weight. You can't fix ugly." But then, standing with the friends who were shocked that my weight had hit triple digits, there wasn't a reason to snap back. Seeing the negative reaction, I decided on the spot that the next time anyone asked, I would lie about my weight, even though I knew that saying a lower number wouldn't change my size.

Now, standing in the store, there was nowhere to hide, and no way to lie. Thankfully, my auntie didn't miss a beat. "Okay, well, you don't have to wear that dress," she said. "Let's find you something else." When it came to her wedding, my auntie saw my size as nothing but a number, and the problem with the dress as nothing but an inventory issue. "Pick any dress in the store. I'll pay for it." Then she held up a dress. "What about this one?"

The hanger in her hand held a dress that was much prettier than the first: deep-blue lace with lots of detail, a bit of a train, and a beautiful silhouette. It put the *bride* in bridesmaid.

The salesclerk smiled. "Great choice. That's one of the most beautiful dresses we have in the store, and we have it in your size."

"I don't want to wear that dress," I said.

My mother nudged me hard, as if to say, *Are you crazy? Your auntie's going to pay for it, and it's prettier. Take it!* But I stubbornly repeated my position.

"I don't want to wear that dress." I carried the ugly size-twelve blue dress into the dressing room, determined to see if I could somehow squeeze into it. My mother followed me into the small room and sat on the bench off to the side, the size-eighteen lace dress draped over her arm.

I put the size-twelve dress on. It fit over my body, but there was no hope of zipping it up the back. Not gonna happen.

"Yetunde," my mother said after a moment, "why don't you just try on the prettier dress?"

"Mom, if I wear that dress, everyone's going to know."

"Know what? What is it that they'll know?"

"They'll know I was the fat one who couldn't fit into the dress." All at once, I sank into my mother's arms, sobbing with my head in her lap.

One of the first things we learn as children is the danger of standing out. Of course, if you know you're a beautiful singer, you might like the opportunity to perform in front of a group. And if you feel drop-dead gorgeous, you might be tempted to wear a bright-red dress to a wedding (although everyone knows you shouldn't steal attention from the bride). When we don't want to stand out, when we want to disappear or hide, it's almost always because we don't feel comfortable or proud of our authentic selves. And that fear—the fear that tells us to be invisible—holds us in place. As young girls we are conditioned to hate parts of ourselves. We spend hours, days, months, and collectively years agonizing over our bodies and the ideal image we wish we could achieve. I didn't want my weight to stand out. I didn't want my dress to stand out. I didn't want to be different from everyone else. I had already experienced enough of that.

I thought about how, six months earlier, I had started high school. It felt like a big change—I was going to be a small fish in a big school. I was nervous, but excited—I'd be driving soon. Would I go to parties? Maybe I'd even have a boyfriend. My older brothers and cousins had gathered in the living room before dinner to figure out our back-to-school outfits and try on our new backpacks. My backpack was already full of all my schoolbooks. I tried it on, and my brothers made fun of me.

"Look at her backpack!"

"It's riding high!"

"What's wrong with my backpack?" I asked, looking around, confused. "It just has my schoolbooks in it."

"That's not how it goes in high school," my cousin explained. "Your backpack can't be that full. It's gotta hang."

"So what am I supposed to do, leave my books at home?"

"Do something. I don't know. Carry some of them in your hands." I reluctantly removed books one at a time until I had their approval.

Then my cousin said something that jolted me. "It's a good thing you're pretty. But they're going to diss you for your weight. In junior high school it's no big deal, but high school is a different playing field. You gotta get that under control."

I knew he was trying to help me, to protect me, but his words sparked an insecurity that immediately took hold and kept growing.

Not long after school started, a teacher called me out for wearing a skirt that was too short. Our skirts were supposed to come down to our fingertips when we held our arms down against our sides. It was true that mine barely passed the finger test, but then the teacher who busted me for it pointed out another girl whose skirt was even shorter than mine: "Hers is shorter, but it looks appropriate on her." Meaning: *She is skinny and looks good in it, so she's going to get away with breaking the dress code. But not you. You're big, so you should hide your body in clothes.*

As a result, I started trying to make my presence smaller, not just in my body but in my behavior, too. I didn't laugh loudly, because then people would notice me and my body. I didn't dance at parties—though I loved to dance—because then people would see me and how big I was. At school dances I told myself that I would dance only if someone asked. I was an extrovert trapped in an introvert's body. I wanted to be part of everything—to dance, to move, to laugh, to goof around with friends—but I held back.

I think any of us would say to that teenager, "Don't worry about it! Go! Dance! Have fun! Enjoy yourself!"—but saying it to young Tunde is easy. What do you say to yourself? Do you stand in your own way, interfere with your own joy and your own personality because you're worried that you'll stand out for the wrong reasons? Is it worth it? To hide our true selves because of a fear that's in our heads?

In the dressing room, my mother held me, finally understanding some of what I had been holding beneath the surface. She took a beat, then said, "Yetunde, if this is something that's important to you, you're going to have to make a change." That was my mother's way. She had never judged my appearance. She had never commented on my weight. She had always told me I was beautiful. But when she saw how upset I was—*that* was what she wanted to change. And she made it clear that I had to be the one to do it. In the same moment that she acknowledged I had weight to lose, she empowered me to change. Without judgment or shame. Just love.

My mother was right. We have to be in the driver's seat of our own lives. Whatever it is that makes you want to hide, you have two choices—learn to love it or change it. We can't let fear steer our course. We left the store empty-handed, but a week later, my mom presented me with a new dress. "Try this!" she said. Looking closer, I realized it was the hideous cobalt-blue bridesmaid dress— and it appeared to be in my size.

"How did you get this? I thought they didn't have my size," I asked.

"I bought two and sewed them together," my mother replied.

I slid the dress on. It fit perfectly. I looked in the mirror and smiled. I was going to look exactly as ugly as everyone else.

At the wedding, I fit in perfectly, feeling the comfortable anonymity of being lost in the crowd. In true African-wedding style, there was no shortage of food or dancing. In fact, most people missed the ceremony and showed up at two a.m. for the dancing. Instead of bringing gifts, it's an African tradition to bring money—preferably in ones—so that you can spray money at the newlyweds. All the little kids crawled around on the floor collecting money and grabbing more as it dropped from the sky. I was too old now to help pick up the money but had graduated to begging my parents for ten dollars in ones so that I could be one of the people to spray money.

After the wedding was over, and all that was left were photos, where my dress blended perfectly into a sea of cobalt, I took my mother's words to heart. If I was unhappy, I had to make a change. I told myself I had to stop eating Whoppers and start working out. My job, working at Fuzzy's Pizza, was next door to a 24 Hour Fitness. When summer rolled around, I bought a membership. It came with a free orientation session with one of the trainers, but I was too embarrassed to be seen trying to learn my way around. I still didn't want to acknowledge to the world that there was anything about myself I wanted to change. I didn't want to admit that I wasn't confident, that I cared about how I looked.

The gym had two sides—one area with cardio machines and another with weight machines and free weights.

The weights area was intimidating. Nobody had taught us weightlifting in school, and it felt like people might watch and judge if I tried to learn here. The cardio machines were easier to figure out without anyone's help, and the people on the ellipticals, treadmills, and bikes were zoned out, listening to music or watching the TVs that were mounted on the wall. That worked for me. We could each be in our own private universes.

All summer, I walked to the gym, worked out on the cardio machines, went to work, then walked home. Without any plan or guidance, I started to eat better, avoiding fast food and sodas. I lost thirty pounds.

That fall, I walked into tenth grade not knowing whether my achievement would be obvious. On the third day of school, I was in the PE room for dance class. The bell hadn't gone off yet, and we hadn't changed into our gym clothes. I always liked to dress up for school, and unfortunately back then it was hard to find stores with plus-sized clothing. Now that I'd lost weight, I could finally fit into the outfits I'd always wanted to wear. My favorite store was called Clothestime. It was the Forever 21 of its time, and I was thrilled that at last I could shop there. That day I was wearing a skintight patterned yellow-and-eggplant off-the-shoulder top with a high-waisted pencil skirt that had a slit up the side and tan wedges. I felt great. I walked across the gym to say hi to the coach. Everyone could see me, and I was strutting my stuff.

Then, the unthinkable happened. Becky Myers waved me over. Becky Myers! She was one of the perpetually pretty, popular girls in our class, and she was acknowl-edging my existence. I walked over to her and her ever-present circle of friends. "You look so good," she told me. "You lost so much weight. How did you do it?"

I wasn't unpopular or uncool—I had plenty of friends in all different groups—the band kids, the stoners, and the popular kids. But I still was not showing up fully as myself. My parents were fighting to make their mortgage in a middle-class neighborhood. I went to a big school where football was everything. (It was Texas, y'all.) I felt singled out enough as one of the only Black kids in my class, and on top of that I didn't have the designer things the rich (and often most popular) kids had. My classmates were wealthy kids who wore the hottest trends, and I bought my knock-off Doc Martens at Payless, where my mom waited for the BOGO sales. Becky was the It Girl. I couldn't believe that someone who I thought had every-thing wanted to know how I did something. She wanted something I had! Did she have confidence issues, too? It immediately humanized her. "I've been eating healthy and working out," I replied.

As I unveiled the new, trimmer Tunde, I continued to get praise from students, parents, and teachers for how I looked. Kids seemed to like me more. I had more friends. I had expected losing weight would improve my life, and it did. Society had showed me that looking a certain way meant I was invited into places.

Before long, I realized that it wasn't the weight itself that had made me hide. Anyone can dance. Anyone can laugh. Anyone can wear a dress that doesn't match. I had allowed my insecurity to imprison me, and even the validation of others couldn't have changed it. What if people didn't start to like me because I was skinny? What if they liked me because I finally showed them who I really was? I had to free myself by being comfortable with who I was.

I felt a new sense of freedom and felt that the world was leaning toward me because I was finally showing up as myself. I allowed people to see the full me. And if I could do it all over again, I'd still get healthy, but I would have allowed myself to love myself before, during, and after. I wish I hadn't waited to be myself.

Years later, when I was twenty-one, I moved to LA. Almost immediately, it was clear that Houston-thin (by then, I had lost fifty pounds) was different from LA-thin. It was on a whole other level. But it was also easier to lose weight there. In Houston, when I was dieting, I'd get together with friends and be the only one at the table trying to find something healthy. In LA, everyone ate that way: green juices, kale salads, kombucha. I lost another twenty pounds.

In those days I weighed in weekly, and during one in particular, it felt like all I'd eaten was air. I'd stuck to leafy greens, vegetables, and water. I'd cut out sugar entirely. I hadn't had any warm, buttery, delicious bread in weeks. I'd upped my workouts, throwing in doubles when my schedule allowed. I knew what I looked like in the mirror.

I should have been happy or disappointed based on how I looked and felt, but instead, the digital scale was the jury. At the end of the week, I expected a reward. The reward was a number.

But when I stepped on the scale, there was no reward. I hadn't lost weight—I'd gained it! It was so frustrating. I couldn't try any harder than I had that week. I went straight back to feeling like that insecure girl who didn't want people to notice she was there. I'd worked so hard for nothing. Not just giving up foods I loved but forgoing other activities to devote time to working out. Sacrificing and compromising, doing everything right in an effort to meet the goal—only to be defeated. I resented the people who had great bodies and never had to struggle, or even try, to manage their weight. Why didn't I get better genes?!

And then, I thought of something my mother had said. *If you want to change things, you have to change things.* I couldn't control the number on that scale. I'd tried and I'd been unsuccessful. But what I could change was the power I allowed the scale to hold over me. It had become the dictator in my house. It told me I couldn't wear an outfit because I was too big for it. It told me I couldn't have fun with my friends because I wasn't on track. I decided to make a change. I wanted to change the relationship I had with my body. I decided that from then on, I would be the one to dictate what outfit I could wear, how much fun I could have with friends, how happy I was. I wanted my spirit to be determined by how I felt, not how the scale thought I was doing. If I didn't feel good, I knew that working out would help me feel better. Lifting weights made me feel stronger. Sweating made me feel cleansed. When I was working out and eating well consistently, I felt better. Rather than fight for a number on the scale, I decided to fight to maintain a feeling. My mother's advice about change hadn't just been about my body. It was also about my mind. We work hard, train hard, and adhere to general recommendations, all to reach an end goal. Yet we don't spend the same amount of time or devote the same type of attention to training our thoughts. It took years to understand that regardless of the way I looked, and regardless of what the scale read, my mind would in the end guide how I felt about myself. **Your mind is your strongest muscle.** It holds the key to your belief about the way you feel and the way you see yourself.

I couldn't make myself a certain weight, but I could make good decisions. I transitioned my validation into activities, things that I could control. I stopped weighing myself.

Ultimately, it wasn't about what I lost but what I gained. I learned how to be the gatekeeper of my own peace, my own energy. I was the one calling the shots. I was the one saying how I felt. My truth was the only one that mattered.

Not the number on the scale.

Not the fit of the dress.

Not the expressions on the faces of the kids in third grade.

Not the words of the teacher who didn't like my short skirt.

Not even the admiration of Becky Myers.

Not any of these exterior voices or measures could tell me how to feel good in my own skin. I was the one.

When truth and trust intersect, you can be your most authentic self. So this is what I want to ask you—when do you most genuinely feel like yourself? Are you alone or with others? Loud or quiet? Dancing or still? And when fear gets in your way—is it because you fear the judgment of the people around you? Or is it your own judgment? While you're on a quest to get to where you're going, wherever that may be, allow yourself to show up as your authentic self. Don't wait for the moment to arrive. **Don't shrink yourself to fit into small spaces. If the space doesn't fit, find a new one.** Being yourself starts right now.

TWO

A Life of Purpose

One day, in sixth grade, I was playing soccer with my brothers in our cul-de-sac when my mom hollered at me to come in. She sat me down and said six words that changed my life: "Now you will start wearing makeup." I was excited. My mom was good at makeup, and I had always loved watching her get ready to go out. She was such a lady. Growing up overweight had made me feel like an outsider, but over the years people had told me that I had a pretty face, and I clung to that. I felt like there was hope for me. Maybe now I could be like her. A woman.

We went up to her bathroom, where there was a long sink with a big mirror. She had a big makeup kit and a magnifying mirror. I pulled up a chair next to her stool, and she showed me how to apply lip gloss, mascara, and blush. It felt special to have time with her—without my brothers—and I liked how grown-up and pretty wearing makeup made me feel. I liked it so much that the very next morning I came downstairs wearing black eyeliner and purple, orange, and yellow eye shadows I had taken from her kit. She had to send me back upstairs to tone it down. Later we would joke that she had no idea what she had unleashed.

I had bushy and unruly brows, and I begged my mother to take me to get them done. I wanted them to be like Pamela Anderson's. On *Baywatch* she had super-skinny arched brows. Finally, before the sixth-grade dance, my mom plucked my brows and took me from a bushy unibrow to a pencil-thin brow that I loved. (Yes, I regret it now that full brows are everything. I'm still trying to grow them back.)

From then on, I played with makeup every chance I got. You would think I was in a challenge with myself to see how many colors I could cram onto my eyelids. When I did my makeup for school, I'd rein myself in, but when I got home, before I washed my face, I'd try out new colors and techniques to see what looked good. Before, I hadn't wanted to be seen. But using makeup was the one way I felt comfortable displaying my personality. One way I was willing to say, "Look at me!"

In high school I begged my friends to let me do their makeup for dances, practicing with their different skin tones and eye shapes. At homecoming, when I was supposed to be paying attention to my date, I kept marveling at my work displayed across my friend Bridget's face. At the Macy's in the mall, I'd walk from counter to counter in the cosmetics department, admiring the makeup and the women selling it. MAC was very popular at the time, and I respected them because they were one of the few brands that made products for my skin tone. I'd stand and watch the artists put makeup on clients. One day, one of them finally turned to me and said, "You'd look so good in red lipstick." He put some on me. I thought I looked like a clown, but I didn't want to offend him, so I walked out of the store wearing it. In the mall, I noticed people looking at me. That lipstick was commanding more attention than any of the makeup I'd been wearing. I thought it was because I looked clownish. Only much later would I come around to the energy and lift that a red lip can bring to a bad day.

Fast-forward to college. I was studying communications at the University of Houston, thinking I might want to be a weatherwoman or a journalist like Connie Chung or Barbara Walters—or, dare I say, Oprah. To pay my way, I was working three jobs, waitressing at a Mexican restaurant, working at a bookstore, and helping out at the college rec center. At the rec center, employees were supposed to wear a red staff T-shirt, jeans, and tennis shoes, but I always arrived wearing the T-shirt, the jeans, and red stilettos. My hair was done in a cute, trendy style, I wore big bangles, and I finished off the look with red lipstick, which I'd finally come around to. I looked so out of place, but I didn't care. I was me. I was free.

One of my bosses at the gym, Ms. Wanda, was always looking out for me. She knew I was juggling a few jobs, and sometimes she'd tell me to go into a back room and close the door, giving me a chance to nap. The building was mostly glass, and from the rec center's office on the second floor she could see me trotting across the gym in my stilettos to get on the elevator. One day she looked me up and down, from head to toe, and laughed. "Why are you working here?" she asked. "Why don't you go work at a makeup counter?"

"I don't have any experience," I told her. "Who would hire me?" The job seemed to require skills that I didn't think I had. It didn't occur to me that I could learn on the job, that everyone has to start somewhere, and that I could be hired because of my potential, not because of my experience.

But Ms. Wanda wouldn't let the idea drop. Back in the day, she had worked for Fashion Fair, a big cosmetics line for women with brown skin, and from the way she talked about it, she had the time of her life there. She brought it up frequently, telling me, "You'd make more money than you expect."

Finally, I went to Macy's in the Houston Galleria to apply for a job. I was just planning to drop off an application, but I dressed for the part, of course. (And my makeup was *always* on point.) To my surprise, the department manager interviewed me on the spot, and offered me my choice of two jobs: a counter manager at Elizabeth Arden or a full-time artist at another brand that I didn't know well.

"Huh?" I couldn't believe my ears.

At first, I thought I'd take the manager job. It was a higher position, and my mother sometimes wore Elizabeth

Arden Red Door perfume. But then I walked the floor of the store and realized that the other brand was younger and hipper. I decided to take the artist gig.

I quickly gained a ton of knowledge about makeup, working with all different faces and all types of products. I also discovered something I loved even more about the job: although I don't think makeup is necessary to be beautiful, I saw how enhancing their features made women feel prettier. I enjoyed helping them find a new level of confidence. A lot. In fact, I fell in love with it. It gave me a chance to listen to people and to connect with them. I tried to understand my clients, and I genuinely cared about them. There's a vulnerability to sitting and getting your makeup done. A stranger is touching your face, seeing those up-close details that you usually only see in the privacy of your mirror at home. The more I did it, the more they opened up to me, telling me about their partners, their hopes and disappointments. I was able to receive and honor their vulnerability. I didn't rush to judgment, and they felt that. I cared about them.

Every human interaction is unique, a moment in time in which we have the chance to understand the person standing in front of us. I couldn't—and didn't—make any assumptions about the people I met. I gave each person the respect they deserved. I always try to do this. Not with everyone all the time—some people have already shown me who they are. But in the line at the grocery store, I give the person who is moving too slowly the benefit of the doubt. She is a human being. Maybe she worked a double shift last night. If a client was rude to me because she couldn't return a product without a receipt, I'd tell myself she might be having the worst day of her life, because otherwise she would understand that I wasn't the one making the rules.

One day, a young woman came in with her mother. She introduced herself as Lacey and explained that she was going through chemotherapy. She had lost her eyebrows and wanted to learn how to use makeup to re-create them. I spent several hours with her, teaching her not just how to do the brows, but how to do the rest of her face exactly the way she wanted it. Sales 101 says that you should spend the minimum amount of time with a customer to get the maximum sale of product, but with Lacey, my only recommendation was a twelve-dollar brow pencil. It wasn't about the sale. Those three hours we spent together were some of the most meaningful of my life. No one should have to go through that—and she was so young—but she had no self-pity. She was optimistic about life and seemed grateful and overjoyed that now she could pencil on her own eyebrows. Right there at the makeup station, we cried together, not out of sadness, but because she was so brave. She had so much light. That day she gave me a different outlook on life and my craft. I understood that I wasn't doing this to make girls pretty. I did it because I enjoyed connecting with people, giving them confidence, and making them feel good. I knew from my struggle with my weight what it was like to feel I didn't belong in the same world as everyone else. An *other*. I liked to make people feel like they were beautiful, like they could fit in without being exactly like everyone else.

When I go into an interaction without any preconceived notions, I can bring my whole energy to the moment. Energy is real. People feel it. You walk into a room and know if people were just talking about you. If you have a crush, you feel the vibration between you. When I interact with a new person, I'm not saying it's the same frequency as a crush, but there has to be that openness to connecting that we both feel. A level of excitement. When you can hold on to that feeling with people, it's refreshing. It feels good. And people respond to it.

After a year of balancing it all, I was making good money, enough to quit the gym and bookstore jobs, so now I just had full-time school, the full-time job at the makeup counter in the mall, and part-time waitressing. The restaurant even let me drop my hours so that I just worked the prime-time hours on the weekend. This was generous of them—some people had to work full-time in order to earn the most desirable hours—but ultimately I knew I had been working hard and had earned it. People went out of their way to help me, but it wasn't because I was cute or nice. They wanted to help me because of the energy that I put out to them. You attract the energy that you are.

I only had a few credits left to do in college when my friends Kim and Kristy, who are sisters, came to me with a plan I couldn't refuse. Kristy and I had met in sixth grade and had been friends ever since. In high school, with four other friends, we'd sneak out of our houses, drive into downtown Houston where all the clubs were, and dance our lives away. When she moved to LA to live with her older sister, Kim, and work as her assistant, I'd kept in touch and visited.

Kim had been competing in beauty pageants and singing competitions since she was five years old. (Kim once competed in a pageant with Beyoncé. So, basically, I know Beyoncé by association.) When she was eleven, before I met them, the whole family had moved from Texas to Branson, Missouri, where for four years Kim sang and danced on stage in two shows a day, six days a week; and when Kristy and I were in high school, Kim competed on the massively popular second season of *American Idol*, and was a top ten finalist before ultimately losing to Ruben Studdard. Since then, she'd been hosting TV shows on popular networks, and over the past two summers, I'd gone to visit her and Kristy. It was surreal. I'd seen images of Hollywood on TV my whole life, and here I was, driving down Hollywood Boulevard listening to music. Palm trees lined the street; the roof was down; the sun was on our skin. I felt like I was in a movie. Kim was maternal and supportive, much more so than she'd been when we were younger. Their friends were cool—some of them were actors I knew from TV.

The second time I visited, we were sitting on the beach in Santa Monica when Kristy told me I should move to LA.

"Definitely!" Kim agreed.

I laughed. "I have to finish college."

"There are colleges here," Kristy replied. I secretly loved the idea, but I laughed it off. I loved my job, had school friends, a life. I couldn't just move to a new city.

When I look back at the biggest shifts in my life, doubt was always there. Think about the times when there was a big shift in your life. I'm going to guess you felt the same. Uncertainty, I've come to learn, *has to exist* to give you room to shift. To make room for opportunity to walk in the door.

It all seemed like a pipe dream until two weeks later, when I was back in Houston and Kim called to tell me she'd found me an internship. She was working for the TV Guide Channel, which at the time had original programming, and had made arrangements for me to assist a makeup artist there. This time I didn't hesitate. School would wait. Maybe I could finish in LA. Either way, it would always be there for me. Who knew if this opportunity would come again?

When I told my parents I wanted to leave college and move to LA, my father was (unsurprisingly) against it. He wanted me to finish college and, like a typical Nigerian parent, wanted me to be a doctor, a pharmacist, or a nurse. But when I asked my mother, she just said, "Okay."

"What do you mean, *okay?*" I asked in disbelief.

She said, "You're an adult. You make your own decisions."

I heard what she was saying, but still wanted her opinion and approval. "But can I go?" I asked again.

"Yetunde," she began, "I don't ever want you to look back at your life and say there was anything you didn't do because of me. If you feel like you should go to LA, then go."

So I packed up all my stuff, hitched a U-Haul to the Ford Focus I'd won in a high school raffle (a true story for another book!), and drove with my friend Devin from Houston to LA. I had $500 to my name, and gas was expensive, so we only stopped once, in El Paso. All the hotels were booked, so we pulled over in a hotel parking lot and tried to sleep in the U-Haul nestled in with my stuff. We were in a dangerous area of El Paso, so we only slept for two hours and got back on the road. It took ten hours to make it through Texas, and we had just made it to Arizona when Kim called.

"Don't panic," she said, "but the makeup artist you were supposed to work for just got fired." I had left college and was using my last dime to make my way west. For nothing. Maybe my father had been right. Before I had time to respond, Kim said, "But don't worry. You have nothing to lose by coming here. If it doesn't work, we'll turn you around and ship you back." I felt like I should be panicking, but she was so confident that it would be okay, I could feel it through the phone, and it rubbed off on me. I was young and willing to take a risk.

Later that day, we arrived in LA. I had $200 in my pocket. Kim's house was on a cul-de-sac, and when Devin and I struggled to park the U-Haul on the curved street, one of her neighbors had to come out to park it for us. Kristy ran out of the house in a rainbow-striped dress and waved a big, glitter-covered posterboard that said WELCOME HOME, TUNDE! in boxy letters. (I would keep that sign in my room the whole time I stayed there.) I had made it. Moving here had been a theoretical concept, but I never pictured it actually coming to pass. People all over the world wanted to visit this place, and now I lived here. LA was for people who followed their dreams, and now I was one of them. I had made a big move. I was a dream chaser. I wanted to own that and do something great with it.

The next day we celebrated my arrival by driving out to Venice Beach. I stared out at the ocean, which might just be the best thing to do when you're making a big change. For so much of my life, I'd been Tony and Tosin's little sister, and then at college, I was just Tunde. College was the farthest I'd lived from the house where I grew up, and it was only an hour away. Now, feeling the warm sun on my skin, I didn't feel entirely like a new person—I felt like the same person, but with a new story.

Sometimes you don't know when you're turning to the next chapter of your life, but this time it was clear. I had lifted my fingertips, turned to a clean page, held the pen, and now I could write out whoever I wanted to be next. I was at a new chapter. I stopped to take notice. I envisioned the blank pages and a pen in my hand. I didn't rush to flip the page and move into something new. I realized how much space I had to create whatever I wanted this to be. The power was in my hands. I didn't want to rush writing it. There was beauty, I realized, in the space I now had.

I decided to take full advantage of the new chapter in front of me. Kim, Kristy, and I did all the crazy, wild things young people are supposed to do. To get into clubs or bars, I'd walk to the front of the line and say, "Hi, I'm a publicist. I'm here with my client, the singer Kimberly Caldwell. You know, from *American Idol* . . ." and we'd get free drinks and a table. But my favorite part was when we would come home at three a.m. and put on fashion shows. We took it very seriously, digging deep into our closets to create elaborate looks and taking turns doing *America's Next Top Model* runway walks from the kitchen, through the den, into the living room. We'd critique each other, channeling Tyra Banks, saying "Do it again, but this time keep your shoulders back. Yes, girl!" Other nights, when *So You Think You Can Dance* came on, we'd put music on and perform our own routines. None of us were trained dancers, but put a few drinks in us and we blew each other's minds. I'd be crying, saying "It's so good." Our nightcaps were always the best part of going out.

Despite my great social life, I needed a job. I called Jenna, my boss from the makeup counter back at the mall in Texas, to ask for help, and quickly got a call from the hiring manager in LA explaining that Jenna had told them they'd be fools not to hire me. I could start on Monday at the Beverly Hills store. I was so grateful and relieved to be offered a job. But when I sat with it, I felt like I'd let myself down. This was what I knew, and it was comfortable, but I had moved from Houston to LA to start something new. Why was I copying a paragraph from my last chapter and trying to paste it onto the clean page in front of me?

Then, something amazing happened. The very same day, I got a call from a woman named Savannah who said she was from a globally recognized top makeup brand—one that I loved. My dream job. Savannah told me she'd gotten my number from the woman I had been planning to intern with at TV Guide. She must have felt bad that her firing had cost me an opportunity and done me a solid. Savannah asked me to come in for an interview on Monday.

I wasn't sure what to do. I knew that the logical thing to do was stick to the plan I'd made to start the job I'd already been offered. I'd worked for that company success-fully for two years already and had made good money. But something had always been in the back of my mind: the company didn't offer foundation in my skin color, so it was hard to feel that their makeup was for me. Sometimes Black women would come up to me at the counter and ask what I had on, and I'd guide them to the best equiv-alent I could offer, but in reality, what I had on my face was the top brand. After all the work I'd done to create those vulnerable, authentic interactions with clients, it felt dishonest—a betrayal, even. It hurt my soul. When I'd left the job in Texas, I had vowed to myself that I would never again work for a company that didn't support me or people who looked like me, that didn't fully embody my values, my beliefs, my community. I didn't want to just take a job for the sake of having a job. I wanted it to be the right fit.

I had never ghosted a job in my life. I couldn't imagine missing my first day of work. But I followed my gut and decided that if I was going to start a new chapter, then I'd let it be new. I decided to go to the interview instead. In the end I got that job—the job I knew, deep down, that I was meant for.

Right away, the company put me through their basic training. I spent five days locked in a room learning everything there was to know about their products and how to use them. I watched the trainer, Cynthia, in awe of her skill as an artist and her ability to command the room. It was her energy. It filled me up. She and the other trainers were giving me something, and I wanted to be the one giving that feeling back to others.

This is what I want to do, I realized. *I want to be a trainer.*

That night, I called my parents and told them, "This isn't a job. This is a career. I can live here and make this my life." They were so excited for me.

I started work at the store in Valencia in the summer of 2007. It was hard at first. I was homesick. I missed my family, my friends, everything that was familiar. When I called my mom, my brothers would be home with her, and they'd text me pictures of them all together. I was missing birthdays and holidays, and often I would think, *Is this worth it? Isn't the purpose of life to be surrounded by the people you love?* I wasn't at all sure LA was right for me, but I told myself to give it a year—and I soon realized that caring people reveal themselves wherever they are.

A few days before Thanksgiving, I got into a friendly

conversation with a random client at the counter and she asked me what I was doing for the holidays. I started to tear up.

"Oh, I'm just staying here," I said. "I have to work, and I don't have time to go home to Houston."

"Why don't you come to my house?" she offered and described a laid-back Thanksgiving with friends and family. At first I was hesitant. It seemed strange, and maybe even more depressing to spend the holiday with a stranger, but Kristy and Kim were going back to Texas to be with their family. All the other girls at the makeup counter were also going home. I was sulking, but here was this sweet woman inviting me into her home. So I said yes, and on Thanksgiving, I made my famous sausage and artichoke casserole and showed up at her house. It was a friendly group of strangers, and I had a great time. LA can sometimes feel young and temporary. In Valencia, outside the heart of the city, in someone's home with a grassy backyard and her kids underfoot, it felt like a breath of something familiar. Plus, two of the guests were local candymakers—their toffee was unforgettable.

As time went on, I was also presented with reminders of why I had made the choice to move to LA in the first place, and why I had chosen my path with makeup. There was one woman we fondly called "The Crow." She always wore the same thing: all black—a black sweaterdress, black stockings, black shoes, and a black hat, and foundation so thick and white it looked like a Halloween costume. Every day she came in and applied purple lipstick so dark it was almost black. It was called cyber. She'd use the tester, then hurry out of the store. After she left, I could see her sitting outside doing nothing.

She always came in and rushed out, but one day she came up to the counter. I locked eyes with her, and we started talking. She told me that her husband, who had died, had loved to see her in that cyber lipstick, but she couldn't afford to buy it.

At the store we would often joke about not taking ourselves too seriously—"We're not saving lives, we're selling lipstick." It was true, but ultimately it was selling the impact short. It was so easy to look at this woman and think you knew who she was. Her story was much deeper than I could have imagined, and I learned so much from her in that short interaction. I saw her every day for nearly two years, but three minutes changed everything. After that day, when I saw her, we'd share a smile.

Another time, I noticed a thin, scruffy white man pacing back and forth at the counter. I didn't know if he was shopping for himself or someone else, so I approached him to ask if he needed help.

He explained that he wanted skincare products, so I gave him a few suggestions. Then, he asked for a little under-eye cover-up. I put it on him, chatting to try and build some trust. Then, he asked if we could even out the brown spots on his skin. Little by little, he asked for more, and by the time we were through, I had done a full face.

Suddenly, I realized: this person was transgender, just

beginning to explore how to present themselves. Before they left the counter, they wiped off the full face. They were going back to work, they explained. I sold them a few products before they left, but for some time after, the visit stuck with me. I was affected by seeing someone come in so fearful and unsure and emerge transformed. For the hour they had been in the store, their shoulders had rolled back, their chin lifted. They loved their reflection in the mirror and felt so comfortable and free. I was witnessing them feel like themself, perhaps for the first time. That, I finally understood, was my purpose: to help them get there.

The psychiatrist David Viscott said, "The purpose of life is to discover your gift; the work of life is to develop it; and the meaning of life is to give your gift away." A key part of our existence on this earth is to share our many gifts. Before YouTube changed the makeup industry, the culture of makeup artists was that you didn't share your secrets. You had a unique style, and that was what helped you book repeat gigs. People knew nobody else could do what you did. But from the start, both as a makeup artist and as a makeup educator, I always told other artists to ignore that rule. It's what we're supposed to do, after all— find what we're good at, what we love, what fulfills us, then use our talents and expertise to benefit others.

I believe we should live our lives in purpose, on purpose, and with great purpose. A life well lived is spent in service. Empathy is the root of service. Imagine what this universe would be like if we all tapped into that?

THREE

Left Foot, Right Foot

My youngest brother, Tope, the baby of the family, graduated from high school in the spring of 2009. I flew in from LA for the occasion, but when I arrived at the school and sat next to my mother and aunt for the ceremony, my dad and other two brothers were nowhere to be found. They were all still coming from work. *I'm saving seats for you,* I texted them furiously. *Where are you? You're gonna be here, right?* Tope was the last of us to graduate, and I had come all the way from LA. Why wasn't everyone making this a priority? I started to get more and more frustrated. People kept asking if they could sit next to us. We held them off as long as we could, but just before the ceremony started, I gave up and relinquished the seats.

Tope walked onto the stage wearing a blue cap and gown. He was one of the tallest in his class with shiny dark skin that lit up on the stage. Tope was different from me,

Tony, and Tosin. Tosin was born two years after Tony, and I was born two years after that, but Tope was five years younger than me, the baby by far. Tosin and I are loud. Tony, the eldest, is quieter, but Tope was his own breed. Because of the age gap, he never had to compete for our parents' attention. Or for the last package of ramen noodles. Even though I was still around, by the time he was a preteen I was out with my friends, doing everything I could to avoid spending much time at home. He had our parents to himself and so was patient and low-key.

In the couple years I'd been gone, I somehow thought time was supposed to stand still back home, and it was a shock when I visited to find that everyone had moved on without me. Tope had grown, gotten his driver's license, and, most recently, had a girlfriend. I loved seeing the two of them together—seeing him give and receive love. But it was hard to believe that he was graduating from high school already. While I was filling in my blank pages and outlining a life, he was writing his own book that I hadn't read. I cheered extra loud, trying my best to make up for my absent brothers and father. After the ceremony, as hundreds of people filed out the doors, my father found us in the crowd and walked up to us. Then Tony and his son, Silas, appeared, followed by Tosin carrying his baby daughter, Temi. Everyone had made it—I should have had faith in them.

My aunt, who always carries a real camera (she's never been seduced by the hype of smartphones), instructed us to pose for a photo. The eight of us stood together in front of the school and smiled. We looked happy and relaxed, but inside, I had a sinking feeling. *This is the last time we'll all be here to take a picture together,* I caught myself thinking as the shutter clicked. It was a morbid thought, but one that didn't quite surprise me. From a very young age I'd feared my parents' deaths, and I had always assumed we would die in birth order, meaning we would lose my dad first. But something about this ominous feeling was different. It wasn't a twinge of deep fear or paranoia. It was a feeling in my gut that this was going to be the last time we as a family took a picture together. So while my aunt was snapping pictures with her camera, I was taking mental pictures that I could hold on to. I tried to take in every moment. I wanted to remember everything.

Two months later, on July 10, Kim, Kristy, and I were back in LA. Ryan Seacrest, the longtime host of *American Idol* and now the producer of *Keeping Up with the Kardashians*, had stayed in touch with Kim and wanted her and Kristy to film a similar kind of reality show called *Crashing with the Caldwells*. We all lived in the same house, so I got roped in as the third "sister." I had just left an hours-long meeting with network executives, hoping the show was going to be picked up (spoiler alert: it wasn't), when I turned my phone back on. Messages and voicemails started streaming in, too many for it to be good news. The first one I listened to was from a cousin, Jumoke, in Rhode Island, whom I hadn't spoken to in years. "I'm so sorry," she said. "Please let me know if you need anything."

I remembered the premonition I had when we were taking the family photo after graduation and felt sure that after all my years of worrying, something must have happened to my dad.

I saw at least a hundred missed calls from my middle brother, Tosin, and a text from him that said, *F-ING CALL ME*. I called him back, and when he answered, he was crying. He was mumbling, couldn't get it out. He just kept repeating, "Tope. Tope. Tope."

"What happened to Daddy?" I asked frantically.

"This isn't funny, Tosin," Kim yelled back from the driver's seat. "This is messed up. Don't joke around."

But Tosin couldn't speak. Suddenly, his friend Randy was on the line instead. "Tunde," he said, "it's Tope. Tope's dead."

"No," I said. "You have the wrong person. It's not the baby. It's my dad." Tope was only nineteen. He'd just graduated from high school. There had to be a mistake. It was just impossible.

Randy repeated the news. Trapped in the peak of LA rush-hour traffic, Kristy and Kim both had tears running down their cheeks. I sat in the back seat, too stunned to react.

We went back to Kim's house in Arleta, where Kristy and I were living, and everyone got to work. Kim called my boyfriend, Brian, to let him know what was happening. Kim and Kristy's mother, whom I call Mama C, booked a flight for me and Brian to go back to Houston. Kristy went to my room and started packing a suitcase for me. I got in the shower, and just sat down in the tub; the hot water from the shower poured down on me. I tried to take a deep breath. Then I burst. My grief finally arrived, and when it came it was loud. I sat there naked, wailing. Kristy and Kim hurried into the bathroom to comfort me. Still fully dressed in their clothes from the meeting, maybe even with their shoes still on, they knelt down and held me. The three of us just sat in the bathtub, weeping.

The house in Katy where I grew up was on a cul-de-sac. It was a blue house with a red door. The cul-de-sac usually provided extra room for parking, but when Brian and I arrived, there was no place left to park on the whole block. Every Nigerian in Houston was paying their respects. Before I went in, I paused in front of the mailbox to look at the big palm tree in the front yard. Mom had planted it from a seed when we were kids, and over the years I'd watched it grow alongside our family. Like the pencil marks a parent might make on a wall to measure a kid's increasing height, this tree had always showed me how much time had passed. Now it was much taller than I was, shading the whole front yard. All four of us, plus two Nigerian cousins, John and Timothy, who lived with us, had been meant to grow with it. The tree stood as tall and proud as ever—it didn't reflect Tope's absence. If that tree was still there, how could everything have changed? I stood looking up at it. I inhaled and exhaled. When

I walked through the door, I knew life was going to be different. I turned to enter the house, but I stopped short when I saw a pearl-white Buick Century in the driveway. A big, ugly car.

Tope's car.

I'd never seen it in person, but I was the reason he'd had it. A year earlier, when I'd just started working at the makeup counter in LA, I'd helped a young woman and a tall young guy.

"Can you recommend an under-eye concealer?" she asked.

"Definitely!" I said and offered her a seat at my make-up station. I found the right color for her skin tone and gave her a mirror so she could watch while I applied the concealer under her eyes. The Rihanna song "Don't Stop the Music" was playing, and I realized I was dabbing on the concealer to the beat of the music. I paused, laughed, and said, "Did y'all realize I was applying this to the beat?"

The couple laughed, and we chatted. Then the guy said, "You have great energy. We work on the game show *Deal or No Deal*. You should come audition for the show."

In *Deal or No Deal*, contestants are shown twenty-six suitcases, each of which contains a random amount of money in increments up to $1 million. The contestant picks a suitcase, which remains closed, so the amount it's been assigned is unknown. Then, in progressive rounds, they decide which of the other suitcases to open, increasing or decreasing the odds that the original suitcase they chose will win them a large amount of money. At the end of every round, depending on which suitcases have been revealed, a banker offers them a certain amount of money to quit the game and walk away, instead of keeping the unknown amount that the original suitcase will win them. Each suitcase is presented to the contestant by a beautiful woman (Meghan Markle once held the distinction). At first I thought these strangers were saying they wanted me to be one of the suitcase girls, but instead they told me I should audition as a contestant. Initially I was suspicious. Before I moved to LA, my mother had warned me about situations like this. She said, "Yetunde, there will be people who tell you they're going to make you a famous movie star or a model. Be very careful." Now that exact scenario was happening. But after talking to the pair some more, I decided they were legit and gave them my number. The show called the very next day and not long after that I auditioned. I had no idea how I'd done until one night when I was at a club, a guy I didn't recognize came up to me and said, "Hey, Tunde. You're Tunde."

"Do I know you from somewhere?" I said.

He said, "Oh, I'm so sorry. You don't know me, but I know you. I work at *Deal or No Deal*. Your picture is on the board at work. You've been selected!"

Months later I finally got the official call. The show flew out my mom, my brother Tosin, and one of my childhood best friends Callye, and I also brought my boyfriend at the time and Kim, who had the added draw of being a familiar TV personality. We went to the studio in El Segundo, and from the first moment, it was surreal—Tosin told me later that when the producers saw that his front tooth was chipped, they said, "Oh, we're going to have to fix that." And they did! They repaired the tooth he'd chipped ten years earlier, chasing me in circles around a gas station in the middle of the night after a Nigerian party. He loved that chipped tooth and wasn't thrilled with the Hollywood intervention, but he did it anyway for me.

The show began, and the first thing they told me was that because the show would air on New Year's Eve, there was a special prize if I made it to the end. What was this mystery prize? It could be $1 million. It could be a new house for my parents.

I started by picking suitcase number 24, which had come to me in a dream the night before. After that, the pressure I put on myself mounted as I played the game—even though it's mostly a game of luck with a little bit of odds thrown in, the money at stake had the potential to change my life and my family's life. My mother had always done a good job of hiding our money issues and I had never thought of us as poor growing up, but now that I was older, I understood the sacrifices my parents had made, and I wanted to give them a break. I agonized over every suitcase because I knew I could leave that day with nothing—or with enough money to buy my parents a new house. At some point I said to Howie Mandel, the host, "This isn't a game. This is real life." The producers were trying to hurry me up—what ended up being a half-hour segment took three hours to shoot.

Early in the show, my mother wanted me to quit, to walk away with a known amount of money instead of gambling on suitcase 24. For the most part, my boyfriend and Kim disagreed. There was so much drama that at one point a producer told me, "I think your mother just won us an Emmy."

In the end, my case was worth $100,000, which was still a huge amount of money for me. I also won the surprise New Year's Eve prize. I have to admit, I was so hoping for a house for my parents that it took me a second to process when they announced I'd won a new car. But there it was, a Ford Flex. I certainly wasn't complaining! The first thing I did when I got the money was send some to my parents to fix up their house. But then my mother said, "Can't you help your brother? He needs a new car."

My brother Tony and I were shocked. "Buy him a car?!" we said. "When did you ever buy us cars?" In high school, I had worked at Fuzzy's Pizza, saved up, and convinced my parents to match my savings to help me buy my first one, a blue Kia Sportage with rims and a sound system. (Tony later told me they'd agreed never thinking I'd manage to save up so much.)

Now Tope wanted a Snoop Dogg Cadillac—a full-sized sedan from the '60s—without doing the work. I didn't want to encourage that. "Tope can get a job just like I did," I told my mother. "I'll match whatever he saves up."

Mom said, "Don't be like that. Can't you help your brother?" My brothers and I felt like as the baby of the family Tope was spoiled. Nonetheless, that summer, my mom called to tell me they'd found a car for him. (He hadn't found a job.) It wasn't a Cadillac but an equally ugly, huge Buick Century. She caught me in a weak moment—two of my friends had just died in a car accident, and I felt like life was short. If there was something I could do for Tope, I wanted to.

In the end, he only had the car for a month. But the last time I spoke to him, he had thanked me again and said, "I appreciate you." I felt a choke in my throat. Those words, to me, were bigger than the car. They meant more than *I love you*. I didn't know that I would hold on to those words forever.

Now, it all just sat in the driveway.

When I walked in the front door of our house, Mom was lying on the couch that Tope always used to sit on, a rose-pink leather sectional with a recliner on one end. I'd never seen my mother sitting there, but now she was in his space, trying to feel close to him. I sat on her lap and cried with her, both of us surrounded by aunties and uncles.

For the first part of my life, my parents had thought that just the three of us would make our family complete. But when I was four years old, we went back to Nigeria and my grandfather begged my mom to have one more boy. She didn't want to, but Tope was born less than a year later. He was my grandfather's wish. I was in so much pain that I couldn't help but think that if it had only been the three of us then I wouldn't have to feel the intolerable pain of losing him. But that thought was surpassed by the feeling that the nineteen years he was here were a gift to all of us.

Losing a sibling is heavy, but while watching my parents lose their child I saw another level of pain. When my friends had died in the car accident, I had spent time with one of their mothers afterward, and I watched her, thinking, *My mother wouldn't be able to handle this.* I had no idea this was coming. Now I understood that I had to save my grief for later. My parents needed me. I needed to parent my parents. It was my turn to put everything aside to protect them. I planned the funeral service, from putting together the program to setting up meetings with the morgue to planning the service and contacting the guests. I wasn't okay, but I pretended to be.

According to his girlfriend, Ashley, she and Tope had been watching *The Dark Knight* upstairs in his room when Tope had said, "I can't breathe." Then, his eyes rolled back. She called an ambulance, and when the EMTs arrived they kept asking her what drugs they'd taken, but they hadn't taken anything. Tope never drank. He didn't even curse. He was always very pure.

When my older brothers, our cousins, and I moved out, Tope still wasn't done with school. He was the only kid left. He became like an only child. After years of noise and chaos, fighting and yelling, it was a very different house. It was clean and quiet. There was nobody for Tope to argue with, and he wouldn't have argued anyway—he had such a gentleness about him. My brothers used to tease him about it. I had actually only heard him curse one time, during a fight when we were kids. He had blurted out, "What the *hell*, Tunde?" My mom, who had been deliberately ignoring the argument, suddenly appeared from around the corner.

"Stop whatever you're doing, Yetunde," she commanded.

"Why are you taking his side?" I asked. "You didn't even see what happened."

"The fact that Tope just cursed tells me you've driven that boy to his extreme. You leave him alone."

That afternoon at the funeral parlor, Tony, Tosin, and I sat in the front row, along with my nephew Silas. My parents weren't able to attend. They were Yoruba, which is the second-largest ethnic group in Nigeria, and in Yoruba culture parents are not supposed to bury their children. They're not even supposed to know where the children are buried. They desperately wanted to say goodbye to Tope, but their friends insisted that they stay home, where they would be comforted by the elders in the community.

Tony, the oldest, thanked everyone for coming, and invited Tope's friends to speak. I hung on to their every word. I wanted to hear who my brother was with his friends. When it came time for the siblings, we all rose and walked to the podium together. Tosin went first. He stepped up to the podium with his sunglasses on, but he could barely speak. Tony put a hand on his shoulder, and I heard him say, "It's okay. You don't need to say anything more. People understand."

Then, it was my turn. I hadn't thought about what to say. The plan had been for my brothers to go first, and they were older than me, so I figured they would take the lead in eulogizing my brother, and once it got to me there wouldn't be much more to say. Now they had both spoken, and it still didn't feel like enough. He was a rare human. A good human. Most of us spend our lives figuring out how to be good, but he was born that way. He didn't need to evolve. This was my family's final way to pay our respects, and my parents weren't there. My brothers had done what they could, but I wanted more.

There is a sensation I get when I am truly existing in a moment, moving in the right direction, driven and inspired. It's like there's a drumbeat. At first the thumping feels like nerves, but as I lean in, it starts to feel like my own heartbeat. Over time, I've realized it's my connection to my purpose.

Every time I had a test or a public-speaking project or an interview, my mother said the same prayer for me: "May whatever Yetunde says be the right thing to say." There was freedom in that prayer, because even a mistake would be right. There would be some reason for it. It taught me to trust myself, so as I stood in front of that room, I started talking. The right words just poured through me. I knew what I was saying, but I wasn't in control of it. I was chanting to the beat in my head. I spoke of his character. How he was good, pure, better than the three of us. He was with us for such a short time—only nineteen years—and he'd brought us so much joy. I wondered if that goodness was why he didn't need to be here any longer. He had been like an angel, briefly blessing us with his presence.

Finally, my nephew Silas stepped forward. He was seven years old. He had never called Tope "uncle"—he always called him "Best Friend." He had absolutely idolized my brother. If Tope stood up to get a glass of water, Silas watched his every move. Now his best friend was gone. He pulled out a piece of paper and started to read what he'd written. "I love you, Best Friend. I miss you, Best Friend. Thank you for playing with me. Thank you for cooking with me. Thank you for being my Best Friend." It was too much to bear, and I could hear that in the room around me. Everyone was sobbing uncontrollably. You could hear every tear, every breath, and in that moment as much as I felt like wailing, I wanted to hear everything Silas had to say. This was a new side of my nephew—he was growing as he went through this traumatic experience. I wanted to be present for it.

It's a fundamental law of physics that energy is conserved, so it's impossible that during the time that followed Tope's death I created energy out of nothing. Throughout life, we choose the memories we store. Moments that seem insignificant gain value as time passes. We save a movie stub, then when we find it in a coat pocket, it takes us back to where we were and who we were in that moment. The moments we preserve—times of joy and struggle—all add up to something, creating a reserve we don't realize we need to draw from until the worst happens.

All my life I had saved memories of my parents' struggle. They kept going, left foot, right foot, left foot, right foot, moving forward no matter what they had to bear. When my mom's father was dying, she went to Nigeria to be with him in his final days, and when she came home, she stepped right back into being our mother again. As a child, I knew she was sad, but I didn't know how to console her. I didn't register how she somehow kept going, but I was watching. My parents felt pain. They endured it. And now I had to summon all that to be there for them. I found a place where I could imagine their hurt, and I tried not to block the pain, but to feel it. To feel the pain they were experiencing on top of my own pain. To ease their burden.

These kinds of moments are the ones where we learn the most about ourselves, and I think that, for many of us, they are when we are most able to grow. Nobody can teach us or prepare us to rise to unexpected challenges, but when necessary, something in us activates the artifacts of strength and truth we've collected in the past to guide us and give us clarity. So take notice. There may be times in life where you're required to call on these moments of pain, so you can step into resilience again.

I stayed with my parents in Texas for three months. The house, which had once been so noisy with all of us, then peaceful with just Tope and my parents, was now too quiet. My mom and I sat on Tope's pink couch, her friends gathered around her. My father sat across from us, grieving. In the first week or two, my brother's car was still parked in the driveway, and one day I found my mom sitting in it. Days earlier my brother had stopped her from drinking water from a Styrofoam cup that Tope had left in the console, baking there for at least a week, but she was so desperate to feel close to him that she wanted to hold the cup he'd held, drink the water that he'd tasted. I climbed into the passenger seat next to her. She was touching the steering wheel where his hands had been.

"He loved this car, Yetunde," she said. "When I couldn't find him, I'd look out the front window and see him in the driveway, sitting in the car listening to music."

I remembered during *Deal or No Deal* how I'd agonized each time I had to choose whether to take the banker's offer or to keep playing the game. That stress had felt so real, the choices so monumental. But ultimately, it was all opportunity. The chance had fallen into my lap, and any outcome would have been okay. The loss of my brother was too real, and it was not okay. I hadn't known I had so little time left with him. I'd been away in California for two years. I would have made different choices if I'd known he was going to die. Now, all I wanted was another option. This car, the house in front of us, the life I was trying to build—I would have traded all of it and more to have him back. I wanted to scream, "No deal! No deal!" Instead, I sat there quietly as my mother sat in a daze next to me.

My mom was never herself again. A piece of her was

gone. A year later, when she, Tony, and Silas came to visit me in LA, I brought them to the beach, thinking that the ocean would be healing, that she could find a moment of stillness and peace. She stayed fully clothed, sitting on a towel wearing a jacket, pants, shoes, and a scarf the whole time. When I suggested she take off her shoes to enjoy the sand on her toes, she said, "How can I do this when Tope can't?"

It took years, but eventually she found joy in her grandchildren. Tony had Silas, and Tosin later moved into the house with his three kids, Temi, TJ, and Tony. The house that had gone from noisy to peaceful to too quiet was filled with life again. In Yoruba culture, they believe that the souls of our ancestors are reincarnated as new children in the same family. The youngest of Tosin's kids, Tony, grew up in my mother's arms. If someone tried to come between him and my mother, he'd nudge his little body between them. My mother never said that she saw Tope in Tony, but I know she found comfort in loving another little boy and holding him close. She tried to be as much of herself as she could be for all her grand-children.

For a long time, I didn't want to talk about Tope. I didn't want to see the sad look in people's eyes and to tell them that it was okay. I didn't want the loss in my life to serve as a reminder that they should feel grateful about theirs. I had to be so strong for everyone else that when it came to myself, when nobody else was around, I wasn't. Kristy and Kim acted as my buffer. They communicated with my work. They managed my life. I didn't recover. Mourning became part of me, but I decided that that didn't mean I had to give up living.

Sam Yo is a Peloton instructor and a former monk. He says, "Life has a way of repeating a situation with a different twist, and being aware of when it comes around again is what helps us to grow and evolve." From my unexpected, unfathomable tragedy, I learned a lot about myself. In life, every moment that we go through leads us to the moment where we are. We lose jobs. We lose loved ones. Friendships fizzle. There are twisted ankles and burnt dinners and infinite smaller conflicts and challenges that we face every day. In the moment, you don't realize that your character is being developed. You're often just trying to survive. But later, looking back, they become clearer. I'd rather have not learned the lesson, but it happened, and in that moment, I could have chosen to be there or to not be there. To show up or to not show up. I'm glad I honored my brother in the most beautiful way. It was the last thing I could do for him. I'm glad I supported my parents and spent time with them when they needed me most. I would give anything not to have lost my brother, but how I reacted? That I would do again. My character is richer and more powerful as a result of the choices I made in my most difficult hour.

You can let your past dictate your story or you can pull from it to create something new. Resilience is the process of adapting in the face of adversity, trauma, or tragedy, having the ability to step up and say "yes" even when you're under stress. My life has required me to be resilient, and I carry what I learned in my most traumatic moments with me in everything I do. We don't choose what happens to us, we choose how we react to it. **Today's a new day; choose to be new in it.**

FOUR

The Blue Light

Seven years after Tope died, I was still in LA, but I had moved to another top makeup brand. I was thirty years old and had landed my dream job as a national trainer, which meant I traveled around the country training hundreds of makeup artists and clients. On any given day, my company might send me out to do makeup for a celebrity's red-carpet appearance or into the field to observe business, meet with store managers, host trainings, and run events to market and sell products. I drove a fancy car and lived in a great apartment in the heart of Hollywood. I had good friends and a great life. From the outside, I had it made. But the truth was, every morning I woke up dreading the day ahead. It was like Phoebe Robinson said: I was "so consumed with 'do this so you can be the best at it'" instead of asking myself if I even liked doing it at all. Time moved so slowly. If you've never had this feeling in a job, well, I'm happy for you! Most jobs have their moments. But when a dream job starts feeling unfulfilling, it's a lot like a breakup. *I thought we were meant for each other! I thought we'd be together forever! How could my feelings change so dramatically?* I was so tied up in the fantasy of my dream job that I forgot to ask myself "Do you even like what you're doing?"

One morning in April 2016, I arrived at a store to supervise a member of my sales team as she coached makeup artists on how to use a new eyeliner we were launching. These were my least favorite trips, because I had to observe and critique the same process over and over again—there are only so many ways to explain the functions of an eyeliner! Before I even entered the store, I had calculated how many hours I would have to endure before I could leave. Within two hours, I listened to eight trainings, one after the next, and all I thought to myself was, *How do I get out of here?* It was too early for lunch—if I went now, I'd never survive the rest of the day, but I couldn't spend another minute listening to this perfectly nice woman describe the best way to get a smooth line. I went into the bathroom and threw water on my face, wanting to wake myself up, to try to care, to summon enough energy to get through the day.

I had taken risks to get here. I had dropped out of college to move to a new city and pursue my dream. I'd worked hard—in my previous job I'd had a two-hour commute and worked fourteen-to-sixteen-hour days with not just a smile on my face, but wearing stilettos and a skintight all-black outfit worthy of a nightclub. One of my mentors had given me the age-old advice to "act as if you already have the job you want," and that defined my work ethic. I was always preparing myself for what came next. I should have been grateful. I was surrounded by mentors who wanted to help me grow and a team who were working their butts off to get where I was—and yet I couldn't imagine spending the rest of my life on this track. Maybe it was normal burnout. Maybe it was seeing Tope's life cut short. All I knew was, when you lose a loved one, life is put in a new perspective. I felt like I was wasting mine.

A couple of weeks later, I was in New York for an annual team conference. My hotel was in Chelsea, and after the first day of events, I went down to the gym to work out. I used my room keycard to open the door, and what I saw was grim. A hot, windowless room with a broken treadmill, a single three-pound dumbbell, and a Hula-Hoop. On the spot, I decided to sign up for a cycling class at a popular studio. Some of my makeup clients had been raving about it, and I'd recently seen a segment from Kelly Ripa on her show, *Live with Kelly and Michael*, that had made riding a stationary bike seem as exciting as a girls' night out in Miami. She described how, at this particular chain studio, they would dim the lights, you'd lock into the bike, and the music would come on. It was like being at a club. I liked the sound of it, so I found a studio near the hotel and reserved a spot in a 7:30 p.m. class with an instructor named, funnily enough, Kelly.

When I walked into the studio, to my surprise, I immediately felt uncomfortable. There was a strong energy in the room, and I wasn't part of it. I was the only Black person there. Everyone else was wearing expensive, matching workout gear and had blowouts. They all seemed to know each other, and they were all very, very fit. Either this was a killer workout, or they were all naturally slim and just came here to be part of this clique. I wanted to leave. At least at the crappy hotel gym I didn't feel like an outsider. I'd come so far from the size-eighteen girl who didn't want to wear a bridesmaid dress that didn't match the others, and I hadn't thought of myself as someone who was afraid to be different in a long time, but it was hard to feel any other way in the moment. I was standing out—and not in a good way.

At the front desk, I was greeted by a fit, bouncy blond girl with her hair up in a perfect messy bun. All her accessories matched. She asked me if I needed a water or to rent shoes. *Did I?* I wasn't sure. I must have taken too long to answer, because she quickly asked, "Have you ever taken a class before?"

No, I hadn't, and I was already regretting the decision. By the time I'd paid for the class, rented my shoes, and bought a water, I was out $40, which seemed like an outrageous price for one class—my gym membership back in California was $48.99 per *month*! I was angry at myself for having gotten caught up in the hype. Maybe if I faked an emergency phone call, they would give me a refund and I could get the hell out of here, but turning around and walking out would have been even more embarrassing—I could only imagine what the cliquey women would say. So, I stayed. *This'd better be good,* I thought.

Messy Bun Woman started handing me things: a towel, a water bottle, and footwear that looked like ballet shoes designed for outer space. I must have still looked lost, because she stepped out from behind the desk and led me to the locker room.

Inside, it was bright and loud. Women from the earlier class were laughing and complimenting each other's rides, using each other's names. To my surprise, there was nothing fake or catty about it—they actually knew and cared for each other. Messy Bun showed me how to program a code for the locker and waited patiently while I struggled with it. We stowed my stuff, and she escorted me into the studio.

It was just as Kelly Ripa had described it: the room was dark with multicolored lights projecting down from the ceiling. We walked to a bike in the middle row facing the podium, and Messy Bun started measuring the height of my hips next to the seat, and the length of my forearms to the distance between the seat and handlebars. She got me clipped in just in time, and before I could ask her how I would ever free myself, she slipped out of the studio. The lights dimmed, and suddenly the room filled with applause and screaming—grown men and women cheering as if they were at a concert. I looked around expecting to see a high-profile guest—maybe Beyoncé or Kelly Ripa. But instead, a tall, lean woman with dirty-blond hair, waving her towel, walked up to the podium. The riders waved their towels back at her. It was Kelly, the instructor.

She introduced herself and cued up the music. Her voice was soothing, but intentional. She knew exactly what she was doing. It made me forget that I was nervous. The first track began, and she started riding. She didn't say much. She didn't tell us what to do. But the room followed, and so did I.

Kelly didn't say anything until the second song, and when she did, it was brief. She prompted a change in pace or resistance, and people reacted. Her phrases were short and direct. Soon I got the hang of it, stopped watching everyone else, and let the energy of the room carry me forward. I didn't recognize the artist or the song. All I knew was that three minutes into the ride I'd forgotten about the $40 investment, had somehow accepted the crotch pain from the bike seat, and was utterly caught up in the music and the motion. I was IN.

It was truly a journey—there were moments when I felt like I was Beyoncé on that bike, slayin' it, and others when I was deep in my thoughts. Kelly said all the right things at exactly the right time. It was as if she knew what I was going through, not just on the bike, but outside of that room, all the questions I had about my life and my future. In the course of that forty-five-minute class, I experienced something I had never expected. I wasn't worrying about what I had to do or planning for tomorrow's meeting or counting how many minutes were left in the workout. My mind had never been so empty, and yet so focused. I was staying in one place, but moving forward, and at high speed had finally found stillness. It was like a moving meditation. When it was over, I felt euphoric. In the locker room after the ride, I looked at the other women with admiration. Now I knew what they were part of, and I wanted to be part of it, too.

After I showered and returned my shoes, I emerged into a foggy, brisk night. The Chelsea streetlights glowed through the haze, as if the whole city was in the middle of transforming from one state of being to another. I'd only gone a block toward the hotel when I realized that my walk had turned into a right foot, left foot, hop. I was skipping, for real! I felt absolutely elated. I tilted my head back and fully extended my arms. I felt the cool mist on my cheeks, still flushed with heat from the ride. The beauty of the city matched my mood. I belonged on this street in this moment as much as I had belonged in that class. And that's when I stopped suddenly and began to laugh. Finally, for the first time in a long time, I felt happy to be alive. That was when I felt the blue light moving through my body. That was the moment I saw my future. *I would be cycling for the rest of my life. And not only that, but I'd be teaching it to others. On the world's biggest platform.* I felt it and I knew it. You know that odd feeling of clarity, that feeling that a thing you are doing is *exactly* what you are meant to do? If you haven't, don't worry. I don't know how often in life we can expect to feel so in tune with ourselves. But it's worth looking out for that feeling, so that you're ready to pay attention to it if it comes along.

It was a voice telling me what to do, but that didn't mean I was ready to just quit my job and become a cycling instructor. I had a successful career. And I had bills to pay. I wanted to listen to my gut, but I also wanted to acknowledge that I'd invested twelve years of hard work to get where I was today. For me, being attached to what I'd already built and not wanting to leave it was a combination of practicality and fear. When your gut tells you one thing and your insecurities tell you another, you have to choose which voice to amplify. The logical, but often limiting, voice doesn't disappear entirely—and that isn't the goal. Acknowledge logic, but turn up the volume on the voice that believes in you. **Trusting your gut is choosing to lean toward the voice that propels you forward.**

As you've probably guessed by now, I didn't tell myself I was crazy, dismiss the blue-light vision, and go on with my unfulfilling life. But also, unfortunately, my blue-light vision didn't cast a magic spell. I didn't become a Peloton instructor after taking one class. I didn't quit my job. I'd always thought it would be cool to work in fitness, but I didn't see it as a daily occupation—maybe as a fun side job at the YMCA sometime in the future. I also couldn't imagine myself ever being qualified to do it. I liked working out, but I wasn't a trained professional. Nor did I have the body. (Remember, I'd been an overweight teen. I'd lost the weight in high school, but I never lost the voice in my head that told me I was too big, that I wasn't good enough, that nobody would ever want to see my boyish body in a sports bra, surrounded by a pool of sweat, at the front of a room.)

I didn't immediately quit my job. But what I did do was message Kelly the next day to tell her how much I'd loved her class. "I fell in love not only with the bike that night, but also myself," I wrote. It was true. In what felt like a moving meditation, I realized my body could move with the music; I appreciated the strength of my big legs; I felt connected to a power higher than myself. I wanted to feel that again, as much as I could, and as often as I could.

When I got back to LA, I went to a dinner party at a friend's house. We ate at a long table. We were drinking wine. And somehow the conversation took a deep turn. I ended up telling them what had happened in New York. "I'm just so certain that this is what I'm supposed to be doing with my life," I explained. Kristy was sitting next to me, as was Max, who was on my team at work and had become my close friend and confidante. He knew how miserable I was at work. The rest of the people weren't as close friends, but as I told them about the cycling class, I started to cry. "I'm sorry, you guys," I said. "I don't know why I'm crying. It was kind of intense. I guess I'm re-alizing that what I experienced was real." Then, to my surprise, Kristy and Max both started crying, too. From Max, this wasn't unusual—he's a person who pulls in the energy of the people around him. But Kristy isn't such a big crier. I was stunned by their reactions. "Wait," I asked, "why are *you* crying?"

"You've never talked about doing anything that sounded more right for you," Kristy replied tearfully. Max nodded in agreement.

I asked them to explain. They both knew I was un-happy at work—I'd told them—but I'd never mentioned the possibility of teaching fitness classes. And I definitely hadn't ever expressed passion about cycling. You'd expect your friends to say, "But you worked so hard to get here!" or "Maybe you were on a high from the class. Maybe you should take a second class before you come to any conclusions." Or they could have said, "You've mentioned going back to school to become an aesthetician—that seems like a more logical next step." Instead, mine said, "We know we've never seen you do it, but it sounds so right."

Kristy and Max were—as Cristina Yang and Meredith Grey would say in *Grey's Anatomy*—my people. In that moment, my closest friends recognized something that I couldn't see myself. In an interview, the Indian yogi Sadhguru said, "Our nose is located right above our mouth. Suppose you don't brush your teeth for three days. Though this nose is right here, it won't tell you have not brushed your teeth. The whole room will know you haven't brushed your teeth, but you will not know." I think about this a lot: *Our nose is too close to our mouth.* We may think we're self-aware—who could know us better?—but sometimes we can't see (or smell) ourselves as clearly as the people around us. Think about that—the moments where you can't see what everyone else is seeing about you. You can't see yourself because you're too close to yourself. This is why we turn to our people. This is why we *listen* to the very few people we trust as much as we trust ourselves. My nose was right above my mouth, but Kristy and Max had been in the room with me, smelling my metaphoric breath, this entire time. When I called it out, they recognized what they had already seen. I had found my calling.

Here's the thing about your calling: it doesn't come with instructions. It's like getting into a car with a destination but no map. You know where you're supposed to go, but you don't know how to get there. So you have to get in the car and just start driving. It's hard to get on the road with so much doubt, but you'll have to surrender to the unknown. You'll have to figure it out as you go. You can ask for directions along the way to make sure you're on the right track, but ultimately your gut has to be your internal compass.

So we had this dinner. We cried. It was very kumbaya. But I was thirty years old, and I didn't know how to make the jump from one career to another. Months passed. I kept going to work, but my job was becoming more stressful. One morning while I was getting dressed for another long day, the local news reported that my daily commute along the 405 had won the number one slot on a list of the top ten worst stretches of traffic in the United States. Later that same day, the company told us that they would no longer be reimbursing us for mileage. I'd now be eating more than one hundred miles in out-of-pocket daily expenses as I traveled to various markets. We were also going through a restructuring, so there were layoffs, and my new territory meant I would have to travel more than the two to four times a week I was already on the road. I got on the phone to vent to Max. I thought he would commiserate with me, but instead all he said was, "Okay, so what's going on with cycling? What are the steps you're taking toward making that happen?"

Since New York, I had been going to a cycling studio called the Sweat Shoppe (now called Sweat Cycle) three to four times a week. It was a heated studio with a diverse crowd where I felt like part of the community, but I hadn't taken any steps toward becoming an instructor. At Max's prompting, I finally decided to take a one-day cycling certification class. It turned out to be a disappointment. I paid some money, took a pretty basic test for which they gave us the answers, and walked away with a piece of paper. I didn't really learn anything about being an instructor.

Then, more than a year after the blue-light experience, I was at a surprise birthday party for one of my friends from the Sweat Shoppe—Carlos, who was in his sixties. His niece Elizabeth was there, as were Angie and Laura, friends I'd met at the Sweat Shoppe. (Like the women I saw the first night I did a class, here I was now part of my own cycling clique.) In the middle of his party, Carlos looked at me and said, "You know what, Tunde? You should teach at the Sweat Shoppe."

"Oh my god," Angie added, "I can totally see that. Have you ever thought about it?"

Had I? "Yeah," I admitted, explaining that I had casually mentioned it in passing once to Mimi, the studio owner.

Everyone had had a few drinks, but we all loved the idea and were in agreement. I had to teach.

"Listen, tell Mimi she's going to audition you," Carlos said. "Tell her you can fill a room. She can put you in at a time when there's no class and you'll fill the room."

I was panicked. Fill a room? I had never even taught a class! "Now how exactly am I going to do that?" I asked.

"I'm going to buy out all the seats," Carlos explained. "Then I'll invite people. You worry about the playlist, what you're going to wear, and what you want to say. Leave filling the room to me. You can email Mimi tomorrow."

I said, "Hell, yeah. I'm doing it!" The next morning my liquid courage had worn off, but I'd committed to asking Mimi for an audition, so I drafted an email. Then I deleted it and tried again. By late in the evening my phone was in my hand, but I still hadn't hit send, when an email came through from Mimi herself. "Hi Tunde!" it said. "The time has come! We're doing teacher training. Are you available to audition for it?"

I wrote back to her instantly, telling her I could make myself available anytime. I'd been taking classes for a year. I knew the culture of the studio. I'd been studying the instructors, the way they spoke, the way they moved, the way they lifted the room. I had more confidence, which to me breeds competence. I trusted my gut and opened the door. To prepare, Carlos helped me develop a workout at a random apartment gym. I also practiced with Latasha, a friend from the Sweat Shoppe who was auditioning, too. I thought about Kelly's class and how it had affected me. I wanted to connect with my riders the way she had.

On the day of my audition, I walked into an empty

studio. Since Mimi had reached out to me, Carlos's offer to buy out a class was no longer necessary. The hot room that typically held fifty riders felt cold and barren. Mimi's husband and our head instructor, Jason, sat alone in the middle of the room. Mimi, holding a notepad, stood off to the side. I was quiet. I knew what I wanted to do. I knew what I was doing. The red light lowered as I pushed start on the track. I began with an unexpected song: "Jusfayu" by KAMAUU. As the music played, I rode silently. I thought about my first cycling class, just before the blue-light experience, about how Kelly allowed the silence to speak. I connected each pedal stroke to the music. The dark room somehow filled with energy and light. Then, when I spoke, I was deliberate. At some point I saw Jason look up at me. Mimi had stopped taking notes.

I was in my space, hearing the drumbeat of my purpose. I finished. Mimi smiled, and said, "Wow, that was incredible."

"Don't say anything to the others," Jason added quietly, "but Mimi is going to have so much fun training you."

I'll never forget the first class I taught at the Sweat Shoppe. I started with "Rhiannon" by Fleetwood Mac, and when the first notes came on, the whole class gave a collective "ahh" of happy recognition. Maybe they didn't expect this Black girl with dreads to play "Rhiannon" as her first song ever, but when they sighed, I knew they were with me. People don't want you to fail. People want you to succeed.

The class's collective *ahh* was affirmation of that. It took the pressure off. My nerves and self-doubt stood down.

From that day on, I stayed after class to chat with the people I was riding with so I could get to know them. Everyone came from different walks of life, but we all loved fitness and could connect over that. That was what I loved most about cycling—it brought me together with people I might not otherwise encounter.

I'd been teaching at the Sweat Shoppe for seven months when a stranger DMed me on Instagram. I didn't know who he was, but I saw he had a blue verification check mark next to his name, so I opened the message. It said he was the director of cycling at Peloton, that they were looking for instructors, and he wondered if I was interested in auditioning. I didn't know who Cody Rigsby was, but I certainly knew about Peloton. By July 2018, the line of exercise bikes with a live and online cycling program had become massively popular. They already boasted more than a million riders and were still growing by the day. The instructors had the reputation of being the best in the business and had dedicated followings. I couldn't believe they knew who I was, much less that they were reaching out to me.

I responded to Cody's message, and we chatted by FaceTime the next day. He was so lively—I could feel his energy through the phone. I thought, *Wow. These people really are as fascinating as they seem on the screen.* I didn't really know what to expect, but the call alone felt like a big step. I knew I would remember this particular FaceTime call forever.

I loved the Sweat Shoppe and my community there. Mimi, knowing that I was looking to leave my day job in the cosmetics world, had been trying to find a way to bring me on full-time. I was ready to take the leap, but Peloton was on another level. If I went to work for them, I could quit my job without hesitation. I could help other people find resilience, help them tap into their own uncertainty in order to expand possibility. I had a message of empowerment that I wanted to share with as many people as I could. This was my chance.

The blue-light vision was coming true.

There were many stages to the audition process, and Carlos stepped up to help again. He, along with a couple of close friends, helped me prepare a taped audition. After reviewing it, Peloton told me they wanted to fly me to New York to audition in person. I put together a short set, talking about my weight-loss journey and trying to convey what I hoped to bring to the classes. Every Peloton instructor is an Avenger, with their own style and energy, and I wanted to show mine. I can be tough, but I'll smile and laugh and dance while I'm kicking your butt. I wanted to motivate people to the next level, to help them do what felt impossible, to inspire them to go further than they'd ever gone. I put together a killer playlist and practiced for the audition at least a thousand times.

Then, at last, I was at the Peloton studio. A woman named Teddy showed me around. Ally Love, a popular instructor whom I knew from my work as a makeup artist, was finishing up a class, so we waited until the room was clear. When she finally came out, she stood in front of a step and repeat—a background that was set up for people to meet her and take a picture with her. There was a line of forty people waiting to take a picture with her. *Wow*, I thought. *This is on another level.* After I finished teaching a class at the Sweat Shoppe, I'd refill my water bottle and chat with the riders about their lives. Ally was being treated like a celebrity. In that moment I understood how big Peloton truly was. People were there from all over the country. I thought of the Leonard Ravenhill quote: "The opportunity of a lifetime needs to be seized during the lifetime of the opportunity." This was a once-in-a-lifetime opportunity for me.

Ally caught my eye and smiled, indicating that she wanted to talk to me after she finished taking pictures. When she was done, she greeted me warmly and explained that it was a big deal that they had flown me to New York, and I should be excited. She wished me good luck and told me to call her and let her know how it all went. I wasn't worried. The blue light had led me here, and I was going to succeed.

Teddy introduced me next to the people in the control room, including a friendly tech guy named Rich. Then she miked me up and introduced me to Shakah, who would be directing the camera behind the scenes. Cody was there to encourage me. Everyone had great vibes, and I felt good. I clipped in.

I wore a blue sports bra with cutouts on the side, and my pants were the Peloton brand, silvery with pink and blue paint splats. My hair was up in braids. I had a bright-yellow bandana around my neck. I'd done my research and knew what the Peloton studio looked like, but now the room that was always full on my tablet looked more like a production studio. There were bright lights and big mirrors.

The drumbeat started. This was the real thing. I was finally there. I was living in purpose, on purpose, and of purpose. *Whatever Yetunde says is going to be the right thing to say.* I had a plan; I had a script; but I didn't have to look for the words. I trusted that they would be there, and they would be right.

I was on the bike, all by myself. The lighting (no joke) turned blue. The music started. "Youngblood" by 5 Seconds of Summer came on and I put us on flat road. I had arrived in this moment, and I wanted to be fully present in it, to remember it. All the nerves I'd felt had passed. The words I said weren't necessarily the words that I'd rehearsed. Rather than letting that throw me off course, I leaned into trust and went back to my mother's prayer. Everything that I said was going to be the right thing to say.

I was feeling good, but I noticed a difference. With a room full of riders, you can see people nodding their heads, looking up to listen, closing their eyes, and taking in what you're saying. You get feedback in real time, and you can adjust the class in real time. In that room, by myself, I had to create my own energy and trust that what I was doing was right. I kept going.

When I unclipped at the end of the session, I felt amazing. Rich, who had been downstairs watching, came in and angled his body so Cody couldn't see him mouth *Yeah, girl!* and pump his fist in front of his chest. Behind Rich, Teddy was beaming. Then Cody walked in. "I'm so proud of you, babe," he said. "That was perfect."

Later, as I walked to my hotel, cars were honking and there was the regular thrum of city sounds. But suddenly, the noise blended into the scene, and I started to see the city differently. This was my city. The streets were mine. The taxis were mine. I belonged on these streets. I lived here.

I couldn't call my own mom, whom I'd lost three years earlier (more on that to come), so I called Kristy, Kim, and their mom, conferencing them all in to one call to tell them I'd crushed it. This time, Kim was the one who started crying. "I'm so proud of you," she said. "I can't believe you're moving to New York. I'm so happy for you and so sad that you're moving."

Next, I called Ally Love. "It went really well," I told her.

"Congratulations!" she said, before a small pause. "I just want you to know if you don't get it the first time around, it's okay," she added. "There are people here who had to try twice."

As soon as I heard it, I pushed the comment to the side. I knew she was trying to be supportive, but she didn't know what I knew. Cody had told me I was perfect! The light had been blue! It had to mean I had the job. I didn't want to seem pompous, so I kept my mouth shut. But I was sure.

On the flight home, I read a book called *Manifest Now*

by Idil Ahmed. It was perfect for the moment. I read the lines, "Affirm: My life is about to change drastically. All that I have been working on and visualizing is about to manifest for me. All my effort and dedication are about to pay off in a major way. I am so grateful, and I feel so blessed to know that everything is happening for me," and exhaled, smiling. This confirmed it. Everything I wanted was going to happen because I'd already seen it.

Cody had warned me that it would be a while before I got the final word. The executives were busy opening a studio in London. Every time my phone dinged, I hoped it would be him. At work, with my phone in my pocket, whenever I felt a buzz, I checked to see if it was news. My whole life became about waiting for word from Cody Rigsby.

Then, two weeks later, I woke up, grabbed my phone as I usually do, and saw that I finally had an email from Cody. "Hey Tunde," it said. "It is with heavy heart that I have to report that our team will not be moving forward with your candidacy for our cycling team . . . I hope you will continue giving this world your light and energy."

Half asleep, I was confused. I couldn't believe it. I'd . . . *seen* it. I had a *dream*. I felt disappointed because I'd had that premonition after my first cycling class. It had been such a clear vision. I reread the email to make sure I wasn't misunderstanding it. I refreshed my phone to make sure another email hadn't popped through with a correction. I dragged myself out of bed, dreading the workday ahead. Imposter syndrome set in. I must not be good enough to be an instructor. Maybe I was too old to learn something new. Maybe it was something I did or said or didn't do or didn't say. Maybe it was the way I looked. I knew loss, and this felt like another one—not just because I hadn't gotten the job, but because I'd been so wrong. From the day I connected to that moving meditation, through two years of stress at a job I hated, there had been a glimmer of light that kept me going. A hum of possibility that I knew was in me. My faith in myself had been misguided. Wrong.

We all carry around judgments of ourselves that we pull out in times of self-doubt. Every time we face something intimidating or scary, these insecurities step forward and say "*I'm* the reason. You'll never succeed because of *me!*" For me, it was my weight. I'd grown up believing that my weight—my big arms, my strong legs—stood in my way. And now, searching for what had gone wrong, I gravitated to that as an explanation. Something had to be wrong with me. If it wasn't my weight, it was something else.

My arms were too muscular. My skin was too dark. When I was a little kid, I didn't hear my mom talk about her image much. I think she knew she was beautiful—she radiated beauty—but one complaint she had about herself was seared into my memory. She thought her arms were too big. She wouldn't wear clothes that revealed them. If she wore a strapless dress, she'd throw on a scarf or a jean jacket, explaining, "Because I have to hide these big arms." She never wore a tank top—it was always long sleeves or a jacket. And so I grew up believing I had the same problem, and that I shouldn't show my own big arms. Like my mother, I never wore tank tops. I couldn't let go of the insecurity that I'd carried with me my whole life.

The self-doubt was just part of the disappointment. Hours felt like days as I went through the motions at the makeup company. It was the same thing every single day. On the best days I'd have a great meeting where I bonded with a client, but for the most part I knew how every day would go, from start to finish. No matter what problem or idea arose, I felt like I'd already heard it. There was no challenge to solve and no idea to feel passionate about. I wasn't learning and growing. This mental fatigue carried over into my personal life. I couldn't clock out of that energy at the end of the day. I felt defeated and it showed.

Ever since I'd seen that blue light, I'd been convinced this was my destiny. I thought I'd seen what was coming, and I believed the age-old saying "You gotta believe it to receive it." I *had* believed it, but it hadn't happened. Peloton had passed on me, and I felt unsure of my path. I couldn't see any way out of the hole I was in.

That week I taught my regularly scheduled classes at the Sweat Shoppe. That place had been my salvation. But even teaching there, which I loved, couldn't give me the same lift. I was disappointed with the news, but I knew there was nothing I could do about it. I had to accept what had happened. I had to surrender. *Surrender.* Just as I had accepted the uncomfortable space of the unknown when it was my choice—moving to LA, pursuing a career in makeup—I now had to be open, to enjoy the space, and to wait for what the universe had in store when it wasn't up to me.

I gradually started to climb out of the disappointment, but my friends stayed pissed—Kim was so outraged that she changed the channel every time an ad for Peloton came on. Still, I wasn't willing to give up. It had been the opportunity of a lifetime, but I wasn't convinced it was lost. I remembered what Ally Love had told me—people had gotten second chances. I had to trust the process. I believe that even when things don't work out, they are working out, and it *will* work out, because everything is happening in your favor. The door wasn't closed.

A month later, I went on a hike with my friend Jade, a confident Black woman about twelve years older than I am with short salt-and-pepper hair, wise from all of the tough lessons life has taught her. "Tunde," she said, "there's one thing I know. If an opportunity doesn't come, it's because something better is around the corner."

"I don't know what's better than Peloton!" I replied. We both laughed, but I believed her. I was still uncertain as to what lay ahead, and that meant anything was possible.

FIVE

A Starting Point

On a sunny afternoon, Kristy and I met at Joe Coffee in North Hollywood. It was my favorite coffee shop— they always put the perfect amount of cinnamon in my oat milk latte. As soon as we sat down, she looked at me. "You're not yourself," she said. "Your joy is missing. What's going on?"

I had tried my best to stay optimistic, but the sameness of every day was wearing me down. After twenty-plus years of friendship, Kristy understands me better than anyone. If I'm haggling with a salesperson, she waits patiently, having long ago learned that I'm going to get the lowest price. She can be at the other end of the room and with one glance know exactly what I'm thinking. If we're at a bar and I'm stuck in a conversation with a guy who's bothering me, she'll swoop in to pull me away. It's as if as my thoughts are forming, there's a scan sending reports to her in real time. She could also tell I was in a funk even if I didn't want to admit it. It's so strange to me, the things we won't acknowledge—but I really didn't want to reveal the true depth of my discontent. So many people would have loved to have my job. My life as it was. I knew that, because I'd been one of them. A career in makeup had been my biggest dream, I'd achieved it, and then I'd been promoted to a high-level position. I'd kept thinking I would be happier when I got the next job, the next promotion, but now I had everything I thought I wanted. Instead, I was increasingly miserable, and I felt guilty over it. Did this mean I was ungrateful?

I looked at Kristy and swallowed hard. "I'm in a dark place. I hate this job," I finally admitted. "I'm losing myself."

Kristy didn't miss a beat. "Well, what now? You have to do something about it. What is it that you really want to do?"

"You know what I really want? I want to work out all day long and get paid for it," I said with a hollow laugh.

She didn't laugh. We've always been each other's biggest fan, and her way of caring about me includes believing in me and wanting to protect me. I'm the one with the muscles, but if we're on a hike and there's a rustle in the trees, I jump behind her. We would take a bullet for the other, but Kristy would be quicker to push me out of the way. She'd react faster. "Well, if that's what you want, if the dream is to get paid for working out, then how can we make it come true?" she asked.

I loved my side hustle at the Sweat Shoppe, but I

couldn't make a career out of that—teaching three cycling classes a week wouldn't pay the bills. I had the same
issue Biggie Smalls describes in the song "Mo Money
Mo Problems." At the same time as I'd built my career,
I'd signed on to a certain lifestyle. I drove a nice car and
lived in a trendy neighborhood. When my friends invited
me out to dinner, I no longer had to check to see how
expensive the restaurant was before agreeing. It wasn't
like I was buying designer bags every week (though I
would have if I could have!), but I'd grown accustomed
to a certain level of comfort I wasn't sure I wanted to lose.
I thought about how my father had worked for years at
multiple jobs that brought him no joy. He'd missed out
on so much. I didn't want to live like that. I owed it to
him to live better than that.

My parents had come to the U.S. from Nigeria in
the '70s after they entered and won a lottery for a diversity visa, which was how most of the Nigerians we knew
emigrated. Dad worked as a taxi driver, a security guard,
and owned a delivery company called Triple T (named
for Tony, Tosin, and me before Tope was born). When
he originally came to the U.S., his destination was California, but he stopped in Texas to visit his best friend,
and the first day he was there he got a job delivering the
Houston Chronicle, so he decided to stay and raise his family alongside his friend and their Nigerian community, to
which he felt great loyalty. Family was everything, but all
he did was work. When he had a break, his favorite shows
were *Martin* and *The Fresh Prince of Bel-Air*, and as long as

I knew him his greatest joy was to lounge in front of the TV in Fruit of the Loom tighty-whities watching them, basketball, football, or the Olympics.

When I was thirteen years old, he briefly went back to school to study chiropractic medicine. I don't know how much of a dream it was, but regardless, he wanted it enough to use his hard-earned money and attend school at night on top of his other jobs. He loved coming home and showing us what he'd learned. "This is L1," he'd say, pointing to one of my vertebrae. "Here's L2, and here are T1 and T2."

Just as he was about to complete the degree, his sister in Nigeria reached out to him. She was having trouble providing for her two sons and was hoping my father could take care of them in the U.S. My mother wasn't happy with the idea. She and my father were already each working two jobs. The house was crowded, and we were struggling. We kept the air conditioner set to 80 degrees to save on the electric bill, and if we left a light on in an unoccupied room, we got in trouble. When friends came over they always asked why our house was so dark. Many times the gas had been turned off, and we had to boil water to bathe (I didn't know that wasn't how everyone showered, I just knew we weren't supposed to talk about it). My mother kept borrowing money from her brother in Rhode Island, then paying it back, then borrowing again, and here my father was talking about taking in two more mouths to feed. It would be a challenge, but our relatives in Nigeria assumed everyone in America was rich, and my father felt a responsibility to his younger sister. "It's my sister's kids," he would argue. "What else can I do?"

My mother understood, but she also knew the sacrifices they'd already made. "We don't even have the money for the plane tickets," I heard her say. She wanted my father to finish school, then use the money that he earned as a chiropractor to bring the boys over. In the end, in order to get my cousins here, my father ended up spending the rest of his tuition money on the flight. That's who he was.

My cousins, Timothy and John, were fourteen and seventeen years old when they arrived from Nigeria. They had grown up in Ondo, the same city my parents came from, but it had come a long way in fifty years and wasn't the same place. My parents had described walking miles and miles to school, across a river, and having to carry water from that same river home in buckets on their heads. My cousins were much more modern than I expected. They arrived speaking English beautifully. They already listened to hip-hop. They were even familiar with *The Fresh Prince of Bel-Air*. We had to show them how to use deodorant and they had to learn to drive, but I realized we had more in common than our differences. John, who was one grade ahead of me in school, showed up the first day and, unlike me, was popular by lunchtime. It didn't take him long to get up to speed on American culture.

Suddenly, I was surrounded by five energetic boys. And all of us except Tony were still in school, which meant we all were trying to get out of the house every morning at the same time. I was the only girl, so I got to have my own room, but when I tried to find some time to prettify myself in the bathroom? Forget it. Getting out of the house to go to church on Sunday, too, was always a nightmare. Someone was showering, someone slept late. We needed two cars to get anywhere. Every day, my house felt like the scene in *Home Alone* where everyone in the family is scrambling to get to the airport.

It was loud, too. In the kitchen, people would argue about food. In the living room, they would watch TV and argue about the channel or the show. They would play video games and argue about whose turn it was. There were always so many things happening all at once, but the noise was mainly good-natured teasing, love, and laughter. And my mother, who had been resistant, treated my cousins as if they were her sons. That was how she was wired. When she went grocery shopping, she bought three gallons of milk, five boxes of cereal, and forty packs of ramen noodles, which we frequently argued about how to prepare. The pantry was piled high with noodles, Hamburger Helper, Kraft Macaroni & Cheese, and Chef Boyardee ravioli. Nights when my mother cooked, the table looked like a Thanksgiving feast. With five boys, a loaf of bread would last all of ten minutes.

Though he never said it, I knew my father always resented not finishing school. He'd had a high level of education in Nigeria, then came to the U.S. and had to work blue-collar jobs. Even after the boys came and settled in, it took him years to admit that he wouldn't be able to go back to school. He always wondered what our lives would have been like if he'd done what my mother wanted.

My father wasn't around anymore to give me career advice (more on that later, too), but I knew what my father would think about me leaving my makeup career— "Keep your makeup job! You're earning a lot of money." He was always much more focused on survival than fulfilling dreams, but I wanted to do it for him anyway. I didn't want to make the same choices. I wanted to live a life of purpose to honor his life of survival. I wanted to live my dreams because he couldn't.

I told Kristy that I was willing to take a pay cut if it meant I could do what I loved. We decided that if I moved in with her and her girlfriend, picked up as many classes as possible at the Sweat Shoppe, and freelanced as a makeup artist, I could make the money work. We didn't figure out my whole life that day in Joe Coffee, but Kristy's gentle prodding took root, and when Mimi, the owner of the Sweat Shoppe, invited me out to lunch, I was ready.

Mimi had just come back from a conference in San Francisco for women business owners, where other CEOs had advised her about the structure of her company. If she wanted to expand, they had told her, she had to plan ahead for the team she would want to support her. That way, she could put it in motion as soon as she was ready.

"I love you, and love you as part of this community,"

Mimi told me once we sat down. "I don't know what role I can offer you, but I want you on my team."

She didn't really know what I did outside of the Sweat Shoppe, so I explained what my job was in the cosmetics world, that I oversaw a territory, training reps to use and talk about our products. As I did, her eyes widened. She'd had no idea of what I did outside the cycling studio.

"Do you think you'd be interested in training my new instructors?" she asked when I had finished. "We're opening a studio in Atlanta. You could train that team and manage their ongoing development. And you could do the same when we expand in LA."

I loved what she was saying. This was a skill I already had, but I could bring it to a different industry. My first reaction was to think that I was too new to train other people, but then I realized it wasn't about being the most senior instructor. As a trainer your job is to get the best out of people, and I knew how to do that, whether I was working with makeup artists or cyclists. I knew how to give feedback and motivate people. Back in Houston, when Ms. Wanda suggested I get a job at a makeup counter, I didn't know why they'd hire me with no experience. Here, I understood what I already had to offer. Being an educator was the core of what I was doing. As much as I loved makeup, my passion was actually in the teaching part. This would be another way to hold on to that. The format might change but the essence was the same.

I was nervous to tell her what I was making. I knew

she couldn't afford my current salary and didn't want to lose the opportunity. But she was a self-made woman, and I trusted her not to lowball me. She'd do the best she could for me. "I know you can't match it, but I'm willing to take a pay cut," I told her.

"Okay," Mimi said. "Give me some time to figure out the financial side of it, but please know that I'm working on making this happen." It was the best response I could ask for. I was back on track, heading in the direction of what I knew I was meant to do. There was hope again.

Before the Peloton audition, I was at a mall in Glendale helping with the launch of a new foundation. I was at the beauty station with my friend and fellow sales rep Billie, demoing the product, when a woman came up to me. I walked her through applying the foundation and she told me she coached women in making purpose-driven change in their careers and lives. She was offering a workshop called "The Accelerator" to help women move forward with clarity and intention. I was interested and asked for her card. Her name was Deborah Bryant.

A couple weeks later, Billie and I went to her workshop at a hotel conference room in Pasadena. There were about ten other women there, each taking turns talking about their career goals and challenges. One woman took the floor and spoke about how she hated her job and wanted to be an artist.

Deborah said, "Why don't you change your viewpoint? What if you look at your day job as allowing you to afford a roof over your head while you work toward being a full-time artist? Recognize that this job that you hate so much gives you the opportunity to have a side hustle."

Sitting in Joe Coffee with Kristy, I thought about that advice. Could I reframe how I saw my job? Not every moment of my work life was going to be rewarding, but if I wanted to stop feeling miserable, I had to look for the meaning instead of focusing on the weariness of another day. To build endurance, you have to endure. It's always difficult when you're in it, but once you see the speck of light at the end of the tunnel, all it can do is get bigger. With time and some distance from the immediate hurt, I could now see things more clearly: before Cody had reached out to me, I hadn't been imagining myself on some Olympic stage or working specifically at Peloton. Peloton was part of the dream, but it wasn't the entire dream. I'd only been teaching cycling for seven months. Instead of feeling like I'd missed out, I should be proud that they even knew who I was. I had to continue from where I stood. I'd fallen in love with cycling, and I was doing it—I was teaching classes. An email saying I did or didn't get a specific job wasn't going to make me happy or change my vision for myself. Someone else's decision couldn't rob me of my joy. I wasn't going to allow it. The choice to find happiness in my work was mine. The choice to be present, to show up in my life, was mine. The choice to pursue cycling was mine. My dream job wasn't going to be handed to me on a silver platter? Fine. I didn't want to feel like I was just passing time. I wanted to honor the process and have faith that it would lead me to the reward. This is what succeeding requires. I loved working at the Sweat Shoppe. I channeled my energy into giving gratitude and thanks to my job for giving me the luxury to figure out what I wanted to do next. Winning isn't about achieving the best outcome; it's the output that matters. All I could ask myself was if I had put out my very best. If the answer was yes, then that was a win.

When doubt arises, we worry. We fear it. I was stuck, but doubt couldn't be the sticking point. Doubt is an internal alert system saying that it's time to shift. **Without doubting where we are, we can't realize where we need to be.** Rather than push it away, we should lean into it. Doubt was telling me that makeup wasn't for me. This was not a catastrophe. I had worked in the industry for fourteen years and loved so much of it along the way. I'd developed a craft. I'd helped people. I'd made friends. It was doubt that signaled that I had an opportunity to find another passion. My body was ready for a new adventure. I could be grateful and still make a change. I didn't know what the change was going to be, but I was on high alert, ready to take my chance when it came.

After a while, I got out of my funk, and I started to take a new energy into my classes. At the Sweat Shoppe when I was teaching in front of forty-nine riders, I walked in as if I was walking onto the Peloton stage. I took each class very seriously, as if I was already exactly where I wanted to be, and I felt joy, engaging with the community. In class I felt the drumbeat again, where my mind and my body were in sync, alive, but also still. I wanted to hear the drum. I wanted it to be loud all the time.

Everything you want is happening right now, I would think. Every moment has led you to this moment. Everything you've gone through has led you to this place and situation. Along the way there have certainly been both missed steps and seized opportunities. No matter what was in your path, you survived, and you landed right here. Knowing that you made it through, trust that you're here for something great. Show up for that. Robin Arzón, Peloton instructor and VP of fitness programming, likes to say, "You've made it through 100 percent of your bad days." None of the bad days have won, even when it feels like they have. If you wait for one day, it may never come. If you give up because you don't have what you want, you won't recognize the opportunity. That's what I saw with my dad. He didn't even bother waiting for one day. He settled for the sake of survival. But if you have your eyes on what you want, then it is already in motion. It's already happening. Don't wait for the fairy-tale moment. It may not look the way you have it in your head. Let go of what you thought should be, and lean into what is. **When we surrender to what is, we lean into our power**. We aren't giving up on our dreams. We're using what we have—where we are—as a starting point.

SIX

Second Chances

On a Tuesday evening in the spring of 2019, I had just left the Sweat Shoppe when I checked my voicemail and saw that I had a message from Cody. "Hey, Tunde," he began. "There's been a shift in our alignment, and I think that shift is in your favor. If you're still interested, I'd love to talk."

If I was still interested? How could he think I wouldn't be interested? But if you looked at my life via social media, I had a lot going on. I was featured in the images they were using to promote the new Sweat Shoppe locations. I had recently been made a face of a new line for a well-known fitness apparel brand and had signed on to yet another potential reality show, thanks to Kim. This one involved drinking lots of wine, so I was game, of course, but it still wasn't Peloton. I later realized that Cody saw what I couldn't—that I had come a long way in the time since I'd auditioned and was well on my way. From the outside, it might have looked like I'd moved on. Often, we're oblivious to how the world perceives us. We have so many hopes and goals and to-dos on the path to accomplishing our dreams that we lose perspective on how far we've come. I thought back to how I'd always felt about opportunity. I called Cody back, and he asked me to audition again.

I was nervous. The first time it had felt like everything was aligned. I had the vision and the opportunity. This time, I knew it could go wrong. I didn't want to risk getting disappointed again. But I also didn't want to go into the audition from a place of fear. I had more of an idea of what to expect and wanted to use that to my advantage. I wanted to magnify the energy, joy, and passion I felt— everything I wanted to bring to this platform. But if there was something I'd done wrong last time, I wanted to fix it. "What should I do differently this time?" I asked Cody.

"Do the exact same thing," he said. "I just need you to be yourself."

I flew to New York midweek. This time, during my audition, I felt less sure. Am I the only person who thrives more in tense moments than in familiar ones? I didn't feel the drumbeat as clearly. After my first audition, I had felt great. I was certain I'd nailed it. This time, I felt good, but not fantastic.

Cody, too, seemed more cautious. When I was done, he came into the room, congratulated me, then asked if I'd changed my playlist from last time. I had—this time

I started with "The Greatest" by Sia. I had also changed my hair. In my first audition, my hair had been in dreads, and I'd since wondered if, in some small part, it had cost me my first chance—maybe my hair was "too Black." I wasn't planning to change myself, but I wanted to start off accessible to the broadest possible audience, so this time I'd worn a simple ponytail. When he had told me not to change anything, I hadn't taken him literally.

Ultimately, I trusted my performance. I didn't go in pretending to be anything I wasn't. I had shown up as myself the first time, and I was myself again. Cody, Ally, and Olivia Amato, another instructor that I'd met through friends, had told me countless times that Peloton just wanted me to be myself, and deep down, I knew they were being truthful.

In my position at the makeup company, I had been part of the hiring process. I could always sense when someone was pretending to be who they thought I wanted them to be. I didn't want to hire someone for a job that only the person they were pretending to be would feel comfortable doing. The people I recommended for jobs were the ones who—even if they were nervous—showed who they truly were. I believed I was what Peloton was looking for. Being myself was going to be good enough. It had to be. If I created some persona, I'd have to keep acting that part every day. I just hoped that the moving parts on their side—the changes Cody had alluded to—would lead to a different outcome this time around.

We all have different versions of ourselves. When we

have a special event or a job interview, we're trying to bring our best self forward. We look as good as we can look and speak as well as we can speak. We shift into a certain mode at work, with family, with friends, and as parents. My friend Jen's mother says, "Grab a coffee and decide what version of yourself you want to bring into the day." But my best self has been, is, and always will be Tunde. It's like any relationship—in the beginning, especially, you try to be your nicest, sweetest, most tolerant self. "Sure, I can wait for you to get ready," you say, or "You prefer that restaurant, okay, sounds great." You agree, you accommodate. But there's a difference between being pleasant and agreeable and saying what the other person wants to hear. If we create some other persona, then every time an opportunity or a challenge arises, we have to ask ourselves, what would *she* do? How would she handle it? For example: I'm not into every sport, so I don't tell the men I'm dating that I am just because I think that might make them like me more. If I did, I'd have to pretend to know what was going on when a game was on TV. Playing that part is exhausting, and we can only pretend for so long. When we show up as ourselves, there is no acting, or worrying about how to keep the act going. We are deserving of jobs as we are. We are deserving of love as we are. The Tunde who doesn't know all the sports terminology is still pretty damn special.

After the physical audition, I had interviews with twelve people over the next two days. The first day, I met with the president of Peloton, William Lynch. Ordinarily, my meeting with him would have come last, but he had to leave town, so I started at the top. Regardless of his schedule, I took it as a good sign that they were having us meet. They weren't going to waste his time on me if I was a dud. I told myself it was already my job, and I wasn't going to walk into his office and mess it up for myself. Whatever I said would be right. Then I rolled my shoulders back and went in. *I already have the job,* I told myself. I was just there to remind him why. I wore a black sleeveless bodysuit and high-waisted black-and-white-striped pants. I wanted to look like myself: polished, but young and fun.

I sat and waited in a small conference room. William walked in, and I was struck by how tall he was. What would I have in common with this suit? But then I found out he was from Texas. That was all we needed. Texans love being from Texas and talking about being from Texas. We discussed important topics like how Tex-Mex is the best type of Mexican food and how hard it is to find queso the way we think it should be made. An hour flew by, during which the only work-related question he asked me was what kind of music I liked. I realized later that he just wanted to know if I was a good fit for the brand, without trying to fit in, without being anyone other than myself. Near the end of our talk, he pointed out the window uptown toward where they were building a new studio in Hudson Yards.

"That's where your new studio will be," he said. I smiled. *I've got this!* I thought.

But I was only just getting started. I was guided from

meeting to meeting, and by the time I got to my interview with Robin Arzón, I'd just finished doing some
screen-testing on and off the bike. I was still in my sweaty
workout clothes, and I didn't even have time to run to
the restroom to put some eyebrows on. I was excited to
meet Robin—hers was the first Peloton class I'd taken,
and I'd never seen anyone so unapologetically authentic.
She cursed during her classes, and laughed, smiled, and
yelled, all at the same time. She was an instructor, but she
was also the VP of fitness programming, had a book out,
and was a brand ambassador for a few notable companies.
Her hair was slicked back, her brows were arched. She
clearly had her act together. I was so in awe.

I met her in a room with tall, clear glass windows. She
was sitting at a conference table wearing her hair in a high
ponytail, a green handkerchief around her neck, a sports
bra that said ROBIN, and a jean jacket. Her presence was so
strong—like a queen on her throne. I walked up and said,
"I can't believe I'm meeting Robin, and I didn't even get
to put eyebrows on."

She burst into thick laughter, and I could see the humility mixed in with her powerful energy. She was cool. *I
can do this,* I thought. We started talking, and when there
was a chance to do so, I asked the question I'd been waiting for her to answer: How did she manage to do it all?

"Tunde, life comes in seasons," she told me. "Everything shifts and changes. I try to get the most out of the
season that I'm in, because I know I'll never get it back."
That motivated the hell out of me. I wanted this to be my

season to teach cycling, to live in New York, to be part of this amazing company. It felt like this was my time. I hadn't been told I had the job, but I felt the change in weather coming.

As she went on, I noticed that Robin spoke almost exclusively in motivational phrases, one line of brilliance after another. I was fighting the urge to pull out my phone—I wanted to write some of what she said down. Later, when I asked her whether she planned out her words of wisdom, she smiled and said, "I'm just calling it like I see it." It was amazing to see firsthand that when she taught classes, she wasn't putting on a persona. That was how she really was. The same was true for Cody. They might have different moods and different energies, but they were playing the role of themselves. It made me want the job even more.

As the two days of interviews rolled on, Cody was my fairy godmother, checking in here and there and going above and beyond to make sure I felt comfortable. I tried to show who I was as much as I could, smiling and laughing and telling stories about my brothers, my parents, my weight loss, imposter syndrome, and the world of cosmetics. When I met with Randy Roth, the executive producer, she praised me for wearing Peloton gear to my audition, and gave me tips on the people I had yet to meet, coaching me on what I should make sure to bring up. My last interview was with Lauren, a producer, who was smiling cheek to cheek as I walked in. "Oh my god," she said, "you have to work here." I felt like everyone was rooting for me.

When I was done, I headed to the airport, emotionally drained but optimistic. After the first audition, I had sat down and ordered myself expensive champagne and duck fat fries before my flight, but this time I wasn't going to get ahead of myself. I sat down in the Uber, took off my yellow jacket, and leaned back. We had started heading across town when my phone rang. It was Cody.

I answered right away. "Did I miss someone?" I said, panicked. "Do you need me to come back? Should I turn around?"

"No, babe." He started chuckling. "I'm so proud of you."

I held my breath.

"I want to go ahead and make a formal offer."

I immediately started crying. "Thank you," was all I could say. "Thank you so much for believing in me."

"I'm so proud of you," Cody repeated, now crying himself. "Thank you for not giving up."

SEVEN

A New York Moment

When I got on the plane, I ordered that glass of champagne after all. The job was really mine. I also called Kim and Kristy. "Man, I don't doubt that you can do anything," Kristy said. "Everything you say you're going to do, you do." I paused to think about that. What she was saying was right. I'd been so busy doing, that I hadn't stopped to acknowledge how far I'd come. Maybe from the outside, it looked easy. It's always easier once you get to the destination to forget about the hills and winding roads you had to take to get there, but I knew—and now you know, too—that there was a lot of doubt and desire and hope all mixed together on the way. The vision had been there, but I didn't know the route I would take. I didn't even believe there was only one. You have to be open to taking any direction, or else when you're thrown off course you won't find the detour that helps you get back on track.

The plan, after all, doesn't always go according to plan. If it looks like I haven't failed, it's because I choose not to see anything that happens as failure. To me, failure doesn't exist.

Imagine that failure is something we tell ourselves exists so we can quit. It's an excuse to give up, to say "Oh, this did not work. I'm done." It creates a limit on what we think we can achieve. Just for a minute, think about what it would be like if we lived in a world where we had no option but to keep trying. If you knew you could never fail, you would never stop trying. You wouldn't have an out. There would be no end line to fantasize about. What if everything we think we're not capable of is an illusion? Then the plan would always be to keep going and going and going. There would be so much more space for opportunity. What possibilities would that space invite in?

When I start a sixty-minute workout, I don't give myself an out. I have already made the decision not to stop until the hour is over. I have to keep going until I fulfill my promise to myself. There was once a day when I couldn't do a pull-up. I couldn't run a mile under thirteen minutes. So I set a standard for myself. **A goal is a wish, but a standard holds you accountable.** I made a commitment to myself that I would prioritize running. Not that I would hit a certain time or speed—just that I would do it. I would run. This in itself felt radical, leaving it open to reach whatever height I could, without something shaping the experience up front. To prioritize myself without thinking of what the result might be. How often do we hold true to our commitments in life with external things that demand we produce something—big projects at work, parental duties, reminders to pay our bills, splitting a check at dinner—and we push ourselves through it just to say we did? We show up for others. So why don't we put that same type of value on the promises we make with ourselves, no matter the stakes? Here's a secret: you will always succeed if the contract is with yourself. It's actionable. It's within your control. You can hold yourself accountable. When you create a plan, pencil in that things may not go smoothly. Then, when you hit obstacles, acknowledge that those, too, were part of the plan. Then you can't claim you've failed. The commitment doesn't fall apart just because something is difficult or goes off course. Your standards change as you do.

Now, even though I don't put much stock in the concept of failure it's still possible to find yourself in a situation where you might come up short in someone else's eyes. Back in LA, I had given notice to the makeup company, but hadn't yet told them why—I had to keep my new job secret until it was announced. Most of my close friends knew I was moving to New York, but I hadn't explained for what. The only big conversation left was Mimi. I alerted her first through a mutual friend, knowing she would be disappointed to hear the news. After all, she'd taken a chance on me. She had hired me with no experience, taken the time to train me, made me the face of her company, and for months she had been actively trying to get me a full-time job. She believed in me. She'd made such an investment in me. We'd had plans. I knew she was really trying to figure out a way to make my dream come true. I felt loyalty to her because we had been a team. People work for people. Part of why I wanted to put my best foot forward was because I loved Mimi. She was such a hard worker. She had put her blood and sweat into this company, and I wanted to show up for her. Now I was leaving before we'd finished executing the plan. It was a very personal relationship, and this felt like a betrayal.

I knew it wasn't a true betrayal. I wasn't leaving for a studio just like hers. I was leaving for a one-of-a-kind, life-changing opportunity. I thought if she understood that, it would help her forgive me. When I called her up to let her know I was leaving, I tried to tell her how grateful I was, how she had given me so much, but she was still upset when the phone call ended. I felt like I'd lost a mentor—more than that, I felt like I'd lost a friend.

Then, two days later, a mutual friend asked me to come over. When I arrived at her house, Mimi was there, and our friend encouraged us to talk. (I found out later she had sat Mimi down beforehand and said, "Tunde isn't leaving for a competitor. This is a life-changing opportunity for her. You have to be happy for her. Take pride in how you trained her.") We did talk, with the friend mediating, and it took some time, but eventually Mimi congratulated me. She hugged me and said, "I'm happy for you. I'm not all-the-way happy for you, but I'm getting there. I get it, and

I would have done the same thing." In that moment, hearing those words was good enough for me. Her forgiveness lifted the heaviness I'd felt.

I arrived in New York on June 30, 2019, not realizing it was the day of the NYC Pride March and the 50th anniversary of the Stonewall riots. Five million people had descended on the city. I got in an Uber and headed toward my new apartment, which was in corporate housing on West 27th Street. We were several blocks from the building when the driver pulled over at the curb. "I can't get any closer," he said. "The streets are closed."

I had two massive suitcases, two huge duffels, a backpack, and my purse. I dragged it all out onto the sidewalk and started trying to make my way to the apartment, walking upstream against the parade through the humid June sun. People were passing out bead necklaces, and I didn't want to say no, but my hands were full, so I just said, "I don't have any hands!" and people started putting beads around my neck. I must have looked a sight, dragging that pile of luggage, sweating and half-lost in the middle of the rainbow festivities. A guy in drag wearing red shiny hot pants and a pride flag as a cape, bedecked in glitter, stopped when he saw me. He said, "Oh, sweetie, do you need help?"

I did need help, but I didn't want to rain on his parade, so I thanked him and kept going.

After about eight blocks, I finally made it to my room,

my white T-shirt drenched in sweat. I was glad that I knew nobody, and nobody knew me. Training started the next day, and with the time change it was going to feel like the crack of dawn, so I needed to make sure I had a solid breakfast on hand. Once I'd dropped all my luggage in my room and changed my shirt, I went to Trader Joe's to get groceries. The layout was completely different from the TJ's I was used to in LA, and for some reason I couldn't find the cheese section. The aisles were narrower than I was used to, and I excused myself over and over again as I went up and down the aisles.

I spied someone who looked like he worked there. "Can you please help me find the cheese?" I asked him.

He pointed me in the right direction and told me the aisle number, but I had been there already. What was wrong with me? Why was this bothering me so much? I'd moved from Houston to LA successfully, without any fear—if it didn't work out, Kim would ship me back home. But suddenly, I could no longer access the feeling that nothing could go wrong, that failure was impossible. I'd left my whole life behind in LA, including my beloved dog, Cesar, who would join me once I got set up. How was I supposed to make this work if I couldn't navigate a grocery store?

I burst into tears, startling the store clerk.

"Oh, baby, what's going on?" I looked over at him. I'd had the good fortune to pick a kind-spirited man. And he was wearing purple tights.

"I just moved here," I struggled to explain, "and this

Trader Joe's isn't like my Trader Joe's. I'm so embarrassed that I'm crying!"

He said, "Don't be. This is a New York moment. You'll remember it forever." Then he guided me through the store, helping me find everything I needed.

The next day, I started training at Peloton. When I first started at the Sweat Shoppe, I had asked Mimi which Tunde to bring to the table: the kick-your-ass boot camp Tunde? Texas Southern charm Tunde? Or super-technical and informative educator Tunde? "Bring all those people," Mimi had advised, "and you'll find a way to blend them as you develop." But the Sweat Shoppe was in LA. The riders there were diverse, but I knew my audience. I'd been a rider with them. I was already part of the community. I'd helped cultivate it. And besides, they were in the room right in front of me. I could see them and feel whether they were connecting to what I was saying.

Peloton was everywhere and everybody. There were maybe fifty people in the room with me while I recorded, but thousands of others were tuning in from home, invisible to me. It felt like the difference between hanging out with old friends and going on a first date. On a first date, you are deliberate about what you do and don't say. You see how the person reacts and know if you can lean into it. On the third date, you reveal a lot more. Eventually, you're farting in front of your significant other.

I understood that they hired people who were authentic and that they'd hired me for being myself—but who the hell was I? I decided to lead with vulnerability and find out. Because there was a screen between us, I wanted to bring us closer by slowly sharing parts of my story. As I got more comfortable, I let the energy I felt on any given day drive the class. I said different things based on what was happening in my world. If I was struggling with my confidence or had a friend who was struggling, I'd bring that topic in. When people say to unpack your bags, they usually mean that you should release the emotional luggage you're carrying for your own benefit. But occasionally, there's something in there that will help another person. That stress you feel over your relationship might give someone else insight. And the positive energy you bring can brighten someone's day. Openness is how we make the world easier for each other.

After my initial training period, I started teaching seven to eleven classes per week. I spent my days at Peloton, and when I wasn't teaching a class, I was reviewing my notes from the last one or preparing for the next one. I'd finish for the day but linger in the office. Robin caught sight of me once and said, "If you're done, you can go home. You're never going to not be busy again. Go enjoy New York."

I tried to listen—but the most I would do was bring my computer and music to a park and work. I maybe wasn't experiencing all of New York, but even after just two weeks, I loved it. It had taken me eight years to say that I loved LA.

Being authentic paid off in unexpected ways. Before I auditioned the second time around for Peloton, I had sent Kim a picture of what I planned to wear. It was a long-sleeved crop top. Kim texted back, *Are you nuts? If you don't show your arms, you're a crazy person.* And now she was proven right. As soon as I started working at Peloton and wearing Peloton clothes, my arms were always visible. People started tagging me on social media, complimenting my arms, and saying they wanted "Tunde arms"! I was shocked. When I didn't get the job the first time around, I thought it was because my arms were too muscular, and now they were considered desirable. *What?!*

Kim said, "I've been telling you this for years." With the help of my community, I slowly shifted my view of myself. It still is amazing to me that at work I'm known for my arms! Even now I still hesitate before I put on a spaghetti-strap dress and have to remind myself that there really are people who want Tunde arms.

As time went on, I began to realize the expansiveness of Peloton. It was more than a cycling company—it was part of people's lives. When you train to be an actor, you spend years going on casting calls, and you know that success means fame—if you land a part on a hit show, you're going to be recognized. You know that comes with the territory. But I wanted to be a cycling instructor. I hadn't prepared myself for how visible my new position was. People knew me. I was in their homes, pushing them to their limits every day. That was a huge and rare responsibility. Once in those early days, I was arguing with my brother on the phone at a restaurant when I saw a family walk past, all of them wearing Peloton shirts. Terrified that they'd recognized me in a negative moment, I drew in my breath and lowered my voice, suppressing the urge to walk up to them and explain, "It's just my brother! We're fighting about which Rocky movie was the best."

Internally, the company was just as invested in the growth of its employee community as it was in its members. There were employee resource groups (ERGs) designed to foster diversity and inclusivity. For the Black at Peloton ERG, I went to a summit in San Francisco where tech companies were recruiting future Black leaders. Soon after that, they asked me to interview the rapper and actor Common at a Black History Month event at the Brooklyn Museum. This was a very big deal. He was a star. I'd never really interviewed anyone ever before, and I was supposed to start with *him*? In front of five hundred people? There was no audition, no training, no practice round. *Why me?* I thought. But I knew what Robin would say to that: "Why *not* you?"

Preparing to do the interview, I started to feel the drumbeat. At first, it felt a lot like fear and anxiety. Logically, I knew that I had the tools to succeed—like anything else I'd done, I just needed to gather information for the first attempt. After I did it once, it would stick. Think about all the times you drive home and realize you don't really remember making each turn or checking your mirrors or coming up your street—but when you were fifteen and learning to drive, you clutched the steering wheel and tried not to blink. You drove down your block at a snail's pace, terrified. Every new skill starts like that and develops toward autopilot. In these moments when you are forced into uncomfortable new areas, realize that all the skills you now have were once new. And the more knowledge you have, the more you ready yourself. Preparation suppresses anxiety. You tone down the voice saying you can't do it and turn up the volume on the voice telling you you're exactly the right person to do it. So, I watched interviews with Common. I read his book *Let Love Have the Last Word* about his relationship with his daughter. He was honest and vulnerable in the book, and I thought about the questions I wanted to ask, how I could draw out what he had to offer in front of an audience. The drumbeat shifted from the nervous pace to the steady pulse of motivation.

The day of the event, I called Kim, as I always did before any big moment. She used to perform, and she knew how to pump me up. She'd always say, "You are a badass. You are smart. This moment is yours. This is what you have to go in and do." But this time was different. She didn't give me her regular pep talk. Instead, she said, "Babe, you don't need this from me anymore. Go there and listen. He'll talk. You listen. If you listen well, the questions will come."

In the museum, there were installations by Black artists on display, and the artists were in attendance. There were also local Black-owned businesses with booths to show their offerings. Before the interview I went backstage and had a moment to speak with Common, who to my relief and excitement was just a regular person. I thought of my mother: *Let everything Yetunde says be the right thing.* And then we went out on stage.

Everything flowed. One question led to the next. I had note cards with me, for security, but I decided to let go and trust my gut. I sat on top of them and still managed to hit every question I wanted to ask. I trusted that everything I said would be the right thing to say.

At the end, I asked Common to answer a speed round of questions, shifting gears from a very serious conversation about his book, which deals with how he was molested at a young age, to laughing over questions like who his favorite artist was and what song he wished was his. It took a certain amount of bravery for me to go through with changing the tone of the conversation—it wasn't necessarily part of what I had planned or what he expected—but I did it. It felt like the interview had reached the right moment, like in class when we'd be doing a climb on the bike, and I'd decide to pull us out of it by flying into a sprint. You would never end a ride with a climb. You have to hit the flat road to wind down. I let go of what I planned and took us from where we were to where I wanted us to be. In the interview, on the spot, I realized that I already knew the rhythm of what I was doing. I'd done it before. The music was his words. I knew when to take us up and when to bring us back down. All I had to do was listen.

In life, when you face the unknown, when you're in doubt, look for the parallels. We all have things we know we can do well, trades or skills that we can apply to new situations. A new mother is tuned in to her baby. She watches its cues and anticipates its needs and wants before it does. If she's taken time off work and wants to reinsert herself, she can use the new attentiveness she's developed and apply that. A teacher has the ability to lead. A nurse has the ability to nurture and can bring that empathy any-where. When we feel insecure, why do we allow ourselves to forget our expertise? You know what you know, and you can carry those skills no matter where you go, into uncomfortable new terrain. Limits are removed, results are open, and failure ceases to exist. When I found a way to bring my two worlds together, I could hear the music. It was there the whole time. I just had to follow it.

EIGHT

The Mirror

Relationships are about seeing others and feeling seen. We give and receive, and it is love that enables this mutual generosity of spirit; we have to nurture our empathy and take care of our needs at the same time. When I moved to New York, my boyfriend Johnny and I split up. It was a hard decision, but I had learned and earned my sense of when I had to prioritize myself. This lesson didn't come easily to me—it came from experiences that, layered on each other, taught me to value self-preservation alongside empathy.

Four years before I started dating Johnny, I'd broken up with Brian. For the first few years that Brian and I dated, we were very much in love. He was a charismatic, likable guy. He was the first guy I introduced to my family, and when he came home with me, I thought he was my person. When I got myself my own apartment in North Hollywood, he moved in with me.

Brian wanted to be an actor and had just signed with an agent. But in the third year of our relationship, I started to see red flags. When his agency dropped him, he was at loose ends. Sometimes he had a job waiting tables, sometimes he didn't. One day I came home from work early, and he was home playing video games. There were dishes in the sink. The trash hadn't been taken out.

"What are you doing home?" I asked.

"I'm off today," he said without looking away from the TV.

"You were off Monday and Tuesday," I said, confused. "They gave you three days off?"

He continued to stare straight ahead. "Yeah, I got fired. I didn't want to tell you, but I got fired two weeks ago."

I was shocked. "Why didn't you tell me?"

"I knew you'd flip out." There he sat in my living room playing video games. I felt like he was a stranger in my house. Had he been pretending to go to the restaurant? What else had he been lying about? And how had I missed it?

Before Brian, I'd been in a relationship with a guy who had been in love with his work. That was his priority. His dog came second, and I was pulling a late fifth place after his family and his friends. I had sympathy for Brian because I thought he had a very difficult childhood. It seemed to me he was abandoned by his parents and stuck in difficult foster placements. He'd been through so much. It was a miracle that he didn't land in a world of trouble. He emerged as such a sweet person. He didn't have a temper or any bad habits. He had come from nothing and had nothing, but he had always made me feel like I was important to him. Brian put me first. After my last boyfriend, that was all I thought I needed. Beyond his lies, I only let myself see what I wanted to see. There was a lot that I was missing. I loved him—but subconsciously or not, he was testing out my kindness. Seeing how much he could get away with. A lot, it turned out. I felt like his mother figure. He was living in my home, paying minimal rent. He needed people to take care of him, and I fit the bill. He wasn't gaining anything because of my loyalty, but I was losing something. It chipped away at me, my self-worth gradually eroding alongside my empathy. A year, then another year, then another year.

I've always been attracted to artists, and I had supported him for a long time. It wasn't about the money, but it looked to me like he wasn't trying to get a job to replace the one he'd lost. He seemed content to spend all day playing video games—we even stopped sleeping in the same bed because he'd play in the living room until morning. Sometimes when I woke up to go to work, he was still there. He claimed he was applying to jobs from home, but I never saw him go to an interview.

When we'd first met, I was living with Kristy and Kim in Kim's house, paying rent. Every morning, I'd get up to go to work and wake him up to tell him he had to go, but he didn't get up. He just hung out in my room. Kristy or Kim would assume they were alone in the house, and he'd suddenly appear in the kitchen and say, "Hey, what's up?"

They pulled me aside a few times to let me know that they loved him, but at times he would overstay his welcome. It created friction in my relationships with Kristy and Kim because while I was trying to be respectful of their opinions, I also didn't want Brian to feel less than.

I kept making excuses for him. I told myself that his hard life had made him this way. I thought it was my job to be the person who didn't abandon him. Consequently, I was the roommate with the loitering boyfriend. One night, I was at a party and my friend Jeremy asked where Brian was.

Joking (though it wasn't particularly funny), I said, "We broke up."

Jeremy was friends with Brian—in fact I had met him through Brian—so I was surprised when he said, "Yeah, it was about time. He's a good guy, but he's not for you." I stood there with my mouth open.

I put my hand to my chest and said, "Jeremy, I was joking! He's downstairs."

Jeremy's entire face and neck turned red. "Damn, Tunde," he said, mortified. "Please don't tell him I said that."

I had thought Brian was still fooling everyone else, but they saw exactly what I saw. A few months later, when I told one of his best friends that I was thinking of breaking up with him, she said, "Thank God." It was more evidence that I wasn't the only one who saw the issues. She said, "Tunde, we love him, but, girl, what are you doing?" She asked me to give her fair warning before

I ended things because she thought he would try to stay with them.

I felt like an idiot. What was I *doing*? It was hard to leave him. I had thought I was going to marry him. His laugh lit up a room. He could talk about anything with anybody. He was comfortable being the center of attention and letting me be the center of attention. He was talented and could have made something of himself, but it seemed to me he was getting in his own way. I wanted to give him a chance to help him find his footing. He had laughed with my brothers, and I'd imagined how well he would fit in with the family. He'd come to my brother Tope's funeral with me. My dad had met him and loved him. And the hardest part was that I felt like my father, who died three years after Tope, had left this earth thinking I'd be safe and protected with him. I knew he'd thought I would marry Brian, and that made him happy. I didn't want to betray that memory.

In the movie *Sex and the City*, Samantha is in a relationship that she wants to end, but she feels like she can't be the one to leave because of all the history between them. "He supported me when I went through chemo," she tells her friends. So why can't she make it work?

"You just compared your relationship to chemo," Carrie responds. I was staying with Brian because he was the person I was dating when my dad had died. I don't know if that means my relationship gets compared to chemo, my dad's death, or death itself, but whichever way, the metaphor wasn't good.

I knew Brian wasn't the one, but still I stayed. After five years, I finally reached my limit. What I saw as his lack of motivation became too much. I woke up on April Fool's Day, 2013, and broke up with him. (I don't recommend breaking up with someone on a day when they think it's just a bad joke.) He didn't have a job or a place to stay, so I told him he could stay with me rent-free for three months. My friends were strongly against it, but he'd told me so many stories about how he'd been abandoned, and I didn't want to be another person to abandon him. I couldn't just throw him out on the street. When you break up with someone, I think it's pretty standard to stop living together, but at the time I was too focused on him.

Three months went by, and he was still there. I kept making excuses, thinking that I was giving him grace. I gave him another week even though my gut was telling me he was taking advantage of me. He finally moved out when I was traveling for work. When I came home, I expected to feel an emptiness in the apartment. But I was so done at that point that all the beauty of the relationship had faded. When you leave a relationship at the right time, you can still cherish the good parts, but when you let it go on for too long, all that you're left with are the messy parts. It was difficult to remember the joy that we once had.

Months after he moved out, I was traveling around the country weekly for my job at a new cosmetics company and just starting to use Instagram. Like most people, when I took a trip, I'd post a photo from the plane, or of my view from the hotel in San Francisco.

Then, I noticed odd things starting to happen in my apartment. I'd come home and find less ice cream than I remembered leaving in the carton, or the TV would be on the National Geographic channel when I turned it back on. I never watched National Geographic.

At first, I thought I was imagining things. I'd had all the locks changed when Brian left. It was impossible that someone was coming into the apartment when I was gone. I was busy and running around, so maybe I wasn't paying close attention to how I was leaving things—just to be sure, the next time I went away, I left the remote control in a specific place so I could tell if someone had moved it. When I came home, though, I was so exhausted that I couldn't remember which clever place I had chosen, so I had no idea if my test had worked.

That Thanksgiving, I posted on social media that I was heading home to Houston. (I have always gone home for holidays when I can, because I want my niece and nephews to have the experience I had growing up of being surrounded by family. I cook the whole dinner—my turkey is the world's best—with corn on the cob, greens, stuffing, cornbread with honey butter, and strawberry cobbler with my no-longer-secret ingredient of cream cheese and Pillsbury crescent dough as the pie crust and top. Two pieces and you're in the ER. Usually when people go away for the holidays they stay through the weekend, but on that particular Thanksgiving, work needed me back by Friday, so I flew home, cooked Thanksgiving on Thursday, and flew back to LA the next day.

When I got to the door of my apartment upon my return, I was shocked to hear my neighbor's TV blaring. It crossed my mind that I would have to let him know that he needed to be mindful of the volume. Then I put the key in the lock, opened the door, and saw that although my apartment was dark, light was beaming across the living room from the big-screen TV. The sound was coming from my own TV. How odd—it wasn't like me to leave anything on before a trip. I walked into the kitchen. I saw a shadow, and then it moved. There was a person in my living room! I gasped. My heartbeat quickened. I grabbed a kitchen knife with shaking hands and flicked the light on.

"Brian!" I screamed.

He was on the couch, sitting upright, with his shoes on and his backpack next to him, watching TV in the dark. I don't know why he was in that position—maybe he heard the key, contemplated fleeing, then realized he'd been busted and decided to play it cool. The fear I'd had one minute earlier settled, and in its place was frustration and outrage. Every ounce of respect I had left for him dissipated. And I was disappointed in myself. This was the guy I had loved?

"Did I scare you?" he said and laughed lightly, as if there was nothing out of the ordinary. He was acting like because he'd once lived here it was perfectly normal for him to continue to enter and exit as he pleased.

"What the hell are you doing here?"

"Why? Did I scare you?" he repeated.

I stomped my foot and clenched my fists. Why was he

not comprehending? I said, "Brian, you don't live here. What are you doing here?"

He laughed again, as if he thought his laughter would quell my rage. Rather matter-of-factly, he told me that he'd used a credit card to let himself into my apartment. I immediately knew that he'd seen a picture I'd posted of me and my niece and nephews at the Thanksgiving table. He'd been tracking my social media and slipping in when I wasn't home for months—ever since I'd broken up with him.

When we were happy together, I had always marveled at how he'd made it out of his circumstances relatively unscathed. But finally, here it was. The damage. He had entered my space, violated my privacy. And yet, I still felt I couldn't blame him for it. He didn't come from a family unit, and he treated his friends like brothers and sisters. I'd been his family, but I'd thrown him out. He had nowhere to go. For a while after that night, through our mutual friend, I kept track of where he was staying—which changed daily—but eventually I didn't even want to know what was going on with him. My empathy wasn't serving me. I had to stop choosing his well-being over what was right for me. I had to remember myself. He had friends, and he was an adult who had to be responsible for himself.

Three months later, the apartment above me became vacant. Every so often I'd hear the Realtor showing it to potential tenants, so I was used to noise, but then I started hearing what sounded like the shower running in the evenings. I didn't think too much of it until one of my neighbors approached me. Brooklyn Jay was a tall, beautiful

Black man with purple braids, bedazzled sunglasses, and shirts that revealed his nipples. He and his boyfriend knew all the building tea. "Ooh, Tunde," he said teasingly. "I see you're getting your thing on."

I looked at him, confused. He thought I had time for that? All I did was work!

Ignoring my silence, he continued. "I see your ex, slipping in and out of here."

Now I was on high alert. *Wait, what?* This could not be happening again. "I'm not with him anymore."

"Girl, it's okay," he said, not understanding. "Your secret is safe with me."

"No, for real," I said. "We're not together. Please tell me what you're talking about."

His tone shifted from teasing to concerned. "I've seen him around," he said. "Definitely."

Oh my god, I thought. The shower running in the vacant unit above me. Could that have been Brian? Was it really possible that he was sneaking into the apartment above me? I wasn't afraid. Brian was not an aggressive person. Clearly, he was just trying to survive. But I felt violated, angry, and frustrated. The next time I heard the upstairs shower running was on a night when Kristy and her girlfriend were picking me up to go to the movies. I told them what was going on, and that I thought he might be there. The two of them boldly went upstairs and knocked on the door. Nobody answered.

While they did that, I texted him. *Brian, people in the building know what you're doing, and they're calling the cops.*

You need to leave. Then we went outside. Moments later, Brian came out from the side stairwell. He tried to pretend he didn't see us and walked right by.

"Brian," I yelled in his direction. "Brian! *BRIAN!*"

He finally turned around. "Oh, hey," he said, as if he had a legitimate reason to be sneaking out of my building.

That was it. I had warned him. My empathy had finally run out. I'd stayed in the relationship too long, making excuses for him, allowing myself to pretend I was stupid. I didn't want to believe this was the person I'd loved, and that this was the person whose love I'd attracted. I had put my empathy for him over my own self-worth. Now, as the relationship flashed before my eyes, I realized he'd been covering up his lack of motivation from the start.

"Brian, you're going to end up in jail!" I yelled. Once again, he laughed it off to downplay the seriousness of the situation. I was beginning to see that attitude as his way of trying to control the situation, but it was also how he denied the truly unsustainable situation he had created for himself. People can only operate within their own circumstances, but it doesn't mean you let them get away with murder. And it doesn't mean you let go of yourself. Brian wasn't a good partner. I could take him on as an empathy project, but not as a boyfriend.

I had extracted myself from the relationship long enough to finally see that the concessions I had made to Brian had taken a toll on my own perception. I felt that this was all I deserved, this man who seemed to be using me for a safe harbor. I was making excuses for him, being understanding of everything he needed, but who was doing that for me? Who was looking out for my needs and emotions? Looking out for ourselves means not accepting less than we deserve—and we don't have to sacrifice that for others. **Once you put yourself on the sale rack, it's hard to go back to full price.** Don't undervalue yourself or everyone else will. That was what I learned from Brian.

Sometimes we need to see ourselves through someone else's eyes in order to have perspective on the moment we are in and what we are allowing to happen. I learned this in a very literal way around the time I was leaving Brian. I received an email out of the blue from the VP of public relations at the makeup company I worked for. She said, "I'm reaching out about something that isn't work-related. A psychologist friend at UCLA runs a support group for young women who come from very difficult home situations. She's looking for positive role models to attend a session and inspire these women. It's ten women ages 18-25. It would just be an informal presentation sharing your experience with the girls. I think you'd be perfect!"

I couldn't believe it. I had just been at dinner with my friend Jessica and had said, "I need to do something that brings me gratitude. I think I want to be a public speaker." Then I showed the email to Jessica, saying, "What are the odds of this?"

But preparation invites opportunity. I wanted a chance to feel gratitude, and I was open to it when it arrived. We have more opportunities than we realize, and the more specific we are in what we want, the more likely we are to recognize it when it appears. Whether you want a promotion or a partner, if you continue to believe it, you'll move into action. I've found that with friendships you attract the energy you exude. It's the same with any opportunity—if you keep putting the request out, it's only a matter of time before it arrives. **Dare to have the audacity to ask for what you want.**

Before I walked into the room in the building where the seminar met, my armpits were sweaty, which always happens when I'm nervous. I called Kim and Kristy for a pep talk.

"You're worthy to talk to these girls," Kim said. "Your story makes you worthy. Those girls are lucky to have you." She was right—I had been a young girl once and that made me worthy enough to share my experience. That was enough. We think a speaker has to look a certain way or have a certain experience. Fixed ideas of how anyone in any role is supposed to look and act weaken our self-confidence. Instead, I focused on what I had to offer.

I went to the group session and spoke to the girls about my job. Then I gave them a little class on makeup application and some free makeup. I loved doing it and told the leaders that I'd love to return anytime they wanted me. So about once every other month I left work early and met with the young women. We'd sit in a circle, and I'd tell them a bit of my story. I talked about being overweight, being insecure, growing up without a lot of money; I

talked about losing my family members; and I always finished the session with a fifteen-minute makeup demo and
some giveaways.

One day a new girl walked in early, when I was alone,
setting up for my talk. She had brown hair, hunched
shoulders, and was wearing a jean jacket. My first thought
was, *Oh my god, this girl is so pretty*. I tried to make conversation with her, but she was very quiet and didn't seem
to want to talk. Soon the other girls arrived, and we went
around the circle, each girl giving her name and age and
how she was feeling. That day, my topic was about how
inner beauty meets outer beauty. As part of an icebreaker,
I asked each girl to say one thing she loved about herself
on the inside and one thing that she loved on the outside.

One girl said that she was compassionate, and that she
loved her smile. Another said she was a good friend, and
that she'd finally come around to appreciating her curly
hair. But when it was the new girl's turn, she couldn't
think of anything to say that she liked about herself. One
of the girls prompted her, and she finally said that she was
funny. But for outer beauty, she had nothing to say. I was
amazed. She was truly stunning.

"Can I say something about you?" I asked.

She said yes.

I said, "I think you have really pretty eyes."

At the end of each meeting, I tried to pick the person
who needed the most support to be my model as I demon-
strated how to apply makeup. This time I asked the new
girl if she would mind helping me out. She agreed and took

a seat in the makeup chair. Her chin was down, and her shoulders were up at her ears. I gently guided her shoulders down and tilted her chin up toward me. I didn't put much makeup on her—just a little tinted moisturizer, a touch of blush, mascara, and a tiny bit of glitter. When I was done, the girls started saying how pretty she looked, and it was clear she didn't know what to do with that. I reached down into my kit, grabbed a little compact mirror, wiped off the inside, and handed it to her so she could see herself. She looked, and her eyes grew huge. She began to cry.

From the bottom of her throat she whispered, "I'm pretty. I feel so pretty."

Here's the thing: I didn't really do anything to her. The makeup didn't transform her. All I did was hand her the mirror she needed. It allowed her to see herself the way that I and everyone else in the room saw her. It's like I waved a wand of belief in front of her face.

I said, "Makeup only enhances beauty. You were already pretty for this to happen."

Finding empathy for yourself is not always as simple as being handed a mirror. About five years later, I found myself in a much more complicated situation, but this time with a friend. Tiffany had been seeing her boyfriend for only a couple of months when we were all at a holiday party with their families. While we were playing Flip Cup, a drinking game, she cheered for another guy when he scored a point. Her boyfriend flipped out and started yelling at her in front of all of us, forcing her into the restroom in tears. Suddenly, we all heard a loud bang come from the restroom. Johnny, my boyfriend at the time, and I hurried over, and I threw open the door to make sure she was okay. As I did, Tiffany's boyfriend stormed out of the restroom toward the parking lot, followed by his brothers, who we figured were trying to calm him down.

Tiffany was upset, but she wasn't hurt. The bang, she explained, had been him hitting the door. "How long has this been going on?" I asked her. *If he did this in front of their families,* I thought, *what is he doing when nobody's around?*

"He's so jealous," she said. "I knew I shouldn't have cheered." But it was just a game. She was on the floor of the restroom, crying, blaming herself. If I was scared of him, how could she explain it away? Despite my concerns, I empathized. My situation hadn't been as severe, but I, too, had formed an attachment to someone who wasn't good for me. I had hoped he would change, wanted to fix him, wanted to save him. I had chosen him over me. I saw shades of the same in Tiffany.

Tiffany started showing up with bruises on her body. She looked unhappy. It was obvious that the situation was not only continuing but getting worse. One time the hood of her car was dented and her windshield was shattered. She told us a story about how someone had threatened her, and her boyfriend had chased him down the street. She spun it as if he was protecting her, but when her coworkers put the stories she'd told together, they were pretty sure her boyfriend had wrecked her car trying to stop her from going somewhere. When she and I spent time together, working out or hiking, I'd see her bruises. She'd say they were from an intense workout session the day before, but I'd never seen bruises like that from a workout.

It was a year later, after they were married, when she called me and Johnny and said that her husband was acting crazy, and she needed help getting out of the house. We'd been in the middle of having drinks, so we got an Uber and went to her house. When we pulled up, Tiffany walked out. Suddenly, there was a flash of movement. Her husband had been hiding in the bushes. Now he rushed after her, grabbed her phone, and threw it on the ground, shattering the screen. Then he yanked her purse away. She struggled to get it back from him, both of them screaming at each other. Her husband was a huge guy, yelling, cursing, his eyes wild and unfocused. He was looking at Tiffany like an animal hunting its prey. I was terrified. I'd had a feeling that she was in an abusive relationship, but seeing his rage that day was more than I could have imagined. I'd never been in the presence of someone so out of control. I feared for her life, Johnny's life, and my life.

"I love you," she cried as he leered at her. "Why are you being like this? I love you."

The Uber driver didn't like what was going down. "Come on," he said nervously. "I don't want to be here. We gotta go."

I said, "Okay, hold on. That's my friend. We're getting her."

"I'm really uncomfortable," he continued. "I don't

want to leave you here. Please get your friend." Johnny started to open his door.

"Don't go out there," I said. "He might hurt you."

Johnny yelled out the door to Tiffany, "Forget your purse! Let's go!"

Johnny got out of the car to try to protect Tiffany, but Tiffany's husband was three times his size, and I got out of the car to try to protect Johnny. "Get back in the car," he yelled. "Now."

The Uber driver didn't want to leave us in jeopardy, but he was getting antsy. Tiffany continued to plead with her husband, begging him to calm down. But I don't think he could even hear her. Johnny led Tiffany to the car, but as she started to get in, her husband grabbed her with his bear-sized hands and shoved her head into the car's glass window. I could hear the door rattling and she screamed. I yelled, "Let's go! Let's go! Please, just let her go!" All I wanted was for us to get away. I grabbed her to pull her into the car. I could see the emotional and physical pain in her face. It was a look I'll never forget. She'd been in this so long, protecting this man at the cost of herself. All the lies were unraveling. I reached across her to pull the door closed after her. Johnny ran to get in on the other side of the car.

We pulled away. Tiffany was crying.

"We have to call the police," I told her. This had gone too far.

"No, please don't," she said.

What? I was in disbelief. She'd just been beaten up in

public. We had witnessed it, and so had the Uber driver. Her relationship had to be over. "I'm calling them," I said, and dialed 911.

Later that night, the police arrested him. That night, back at our apartment, she told us everything. In the next few weeks, she and I became closer. We spent time hiking, and on those hikes we talked. When it came to her husband, she felt guilt around sending him to jail. We talked mostly about her, though, and her past relationships, and I started to see how hard it was for her to see her own value. She was determined to heal herself.

But when the time came, Tiffany appeared in court and defended her husband. They ended up getting back together. I didn't see that coming, and it was difficult for me to understand and accept. I felt like we'd all been in the same violent situation. If he'd had a gun that night, I believe he would have used it. Her going back to him felt like acceptance of how he had behaved. There are all kinds of reasons it can be difficult to extract oneself from an abusive relationship. I didn't want her to be stuck there forever, but she wasn't ready to leave. It was heartbreaking that Johnny and I couldn't get through to her, and it showed me how nuanced and complicated domestic violence is. I wanted to use what I'd learned to help her. I had made excuses just like she did and, seeing my relationship through friends' eyes had helped me. But my situation was very different and far less dangerous. She had to find her power on her own.

Sometime after, she finally left him. When she called

me, she said, "I lost all of my friends because I chose him over them. I have nobody." I saw her realize not only the mistake, but what the mistake had cost her. She had chosen violence over love because of her own insecurities. She didn't need forgiveness from her friends. She needed to understand and forgive herself. Much as I cared about her, I had to withdraw from our friendship when I wasn't safe, but my empathy for her never diminished, and it was waiting for her when she was ready to receive it.

When I worked with the abused girls, I held a mirror up to them to help them see their own beauty. For the girl I told you about, it helped her see that she was beautiful through others' eyes. With Brian, I had to hold up a mirror to myself to see that I was enabling his behavior, to see that I was worth more than the way he was treating me. With Tiffany, I tried to hold a mirror up to her—so did other friends and family members—but it didn't work until she was ready to see herself.

As a teacher, I hold the mirror up to myself and look for ways to help people hold a mirror up to themselves. In class, I talk about adding resistance to the bike, pushing through it, and getting to the other side of the effort. I'll say, "I know this part is challenging, but you can do it." I may sound like I'm simply trying to give people a good workout, but it's always about more than the ride. **We hear what we need to hear when we need to hear it.** You know how it is when there's an old love song you've heard hundreds of times, but one day it comes on and it hits exactly how you feel? I watch people repost quotes from the rides they've done, and I see that different language resonates with different people at different times. One time a rider wrote me a long note about how much it meant to her when I used the word "prepare." That was what she needed in that moment. Some people might only hear instructions for the bike because nothing connects to what they're going through, but I always keep in mind that a Tiffany or a Brian or a younger Tunde might be in my class. I hope they can find the space to extract something they're able to use. In class I say, "Don't feel selfish about taking the time to work out." Someone feels like they should be packing their kids' bag for school tomorrow. Someone else is in the middle of a special project for their boss. But taking care of yourself is important, too.

When I left LA and my relationship to come to New York, I allowed myself to be selfish. Or maybe I allowed myself to be self-full. I knew what this opportunity meant to me. I knew I had to focus on myself. I allowed myself to acknowledge that and to be okay with it. I was finally holding the mirror up to myself, seeing exactly where I'd been and what I needed.

NINE

Speak Up

On May 25, 2020, George Floyd was murdered in police custody. This happens to any number of Black Americans, but this was one of the instances when it actually was caught on tape, and so this time people paid attention. At work that day, people were saying not to watch the video, that it was too upsetting, but by the end of the day, I knew I needed to see it. Like the rest of the world, I watched it. It was gut-wrenching—awful to watch but impossible to turn away. I watched it more than once, each time feeling a different emotion. I was sad. I was disgusted. I was enraged. Why did this continue to happen? I had no words. I felt hopeless and helpless. I didn't know what to do with myself. I couldn't just carry on with my day. I donated to Black Lives Matter. I read books about racism in America. I went to a small protest up in Harlem. Nothing would ever be enough.

Houston is home to the largest Nigerian community in the U.S. I wasn't born in Nigeria—I am an American who grew up in a culturally African household. My parents made a point of exposing me to my roots. There was no Luther Vandross for us—we grew up listening to the Nigerian pop star King Sunny Ade. As I got older, I tried to learn what I had missed about Black culture having grown up in an African family, but now the two cultures have merged for me. When my parents came to this country, they raised their children in an inherited culture of oppression the same way white people have inherited a culture of privilege. I have seen it firsthand.

When I was in elementary school, for example, I idolized my teachers—I wanted to be one when I grew up. In third grade I wanted to be my teacher, Mrs. Cunningham's, favorite. She used a wheelchair, and she'd let people push her when we went to lunch, PE, and recess. I really wanted to have a turn at pushing her, but she always told me I couldn't. "You don't know how," she explained.

I thought I needed to watch and learn. It didn't occur to me that the other kids who were allowed to push her had started school at the same time as I did, that they had learned because she let them try. For some reason, she never gave me the same chance. But I kept asking every day, certain my turn would come. Then, more than half-way through the year, a new kid joined our class. When he asked Mrs. Cunningham if he could push her, she said yes. It was only his second or third day of school! I didn't know the reason for it, but I felt the injustice of it deeply. My teacher didn't like me—she was always nasty to me—but I had no idea why. I'll never forget that feeling.

Later, I overheard my brothers talking about her being racist. I knew racism as something my dad talked about with his friends or a word that I heard when my mom was watching Oprah. But now I realized that it had just happened to me. It was a reality, not just a thought or concept—and I was going to have to look at people differently now and think about how they might see me.

My school was mostly white, and when we learned about slavery, I was the only Black person in the room. People turned around to look at me as they realized that someone who looked like me would have been a slave 120 years earlier. We were young, but we were already realizing that I held a different position in our country because of my skin color.

Discomfort turned to danger when I was sixteen or seventeen, and I was driving with my brother Tosin, listening to music, speeding. A cop pulled us over, and when she came to the window, she told us we'd been going 50 in a 35 mph zone. I couldn't believe I'd been going so fast. I wasn't even on the freeway.

"I'm so sorry," I said.

"I'm going to need to see your license," she replied. I gave it to her, and she went back to her car. We waited for a long time, and then suddenly another cop car pulled up.

"Tunde," Tosin said from the passenger seat, "when they come back, say 'Yes, sir. Yes, ma'am' and 'No, sir. No, ma'am.' That's it. That's all you say." He knew that I was the type to ask questions. I had an education and an opinion, and was never afraid to speak my mind in any situation. "This is not the time to debate," he reminded me, looking at me sternly. I knew I should take him seriously.

The cop still hadn't returned to our car when a third cop car arrived, then a fourth. The first cop finally came back to our car. "What are you doing in this neighborhood?" she asked with a sneer.

I was wearing a Taylor High School T-shirt. I pointed at it. "I live here," I said.

"When was the last time you smoked weed?"

What? I had never even tried it. "I don't smoke weed, ma'am," I replied, as respectfully as possible.

"We smell weed. Get out of the car."

Through it all, I noticed my brother was being very polite. He kept his hands out in front of him—not scratching his head or moving at all. "Everything's going to be fine," he told me. "Just do whatever she asks."

We had moved from Houston to Katy, a suburb, because my mother was worried about my brothers growing up in the city. They were six and eight and were transitioning from being cute to the age where people might feel threatened by them. My mother hadn't grown up with systemic racism—in Nigeria, lines are drawn by class, not color—but my parents knew what went on in America and understood that while there was great opportunity here, we had to remember who we were and what we looked like in the world.

My parents worried that my brothers and cousins would

be targeted or get caught up with bad people. I overheard them give them "the talk": *Don't run from a police officer. Always show your hands. Always say 'yes, sir' and 'no, sir.' You can't do what your friends do. You need to be mindful of what you do and what you say because of the color of your skin. Because I want you to get home safely.*

We sat down on the curb with our hands behind our backs while the police searched my car. We were near the parking lot of a Blockbuster, and a small crowd had gathered to see what was going on. I was embarrassed—there were four cop cars! Then, the cop pulled a bag out of the car. "Got it," she said victoriously. They looked inside. It was just a bag of coins.

"Okay, we're done here," one of the cops said.

I was upset. I had been naïve enough to think that I wouldn't be racially profiled. Maybe it was because in general we assume things that are in the news won't happen to us, or maybe I thought it only happened to Black men. I hated the idea that the people standing around might assume we were guilty of something. This was my neighborhood. People recognized me. None of them were going to forget the image of me and my brother with our hands behind us as our car was being searched. I said to the cop, "This was so embarrassing. If I got a ticket, why didn't you just give me a ticket?"

Tosin said, "Tunde, shut up. Let's go."

"Can I get an apology?" I continued indignantly, ignoring my brother. "You said you smelled weed. And before you searched the car you called for backup."

"It doesn't matter, Tunde, just get in the car," Tosin said.

"If I were you, I'd listen to your brother," the officer added.

I stopped talking. She handed me a ticket and went on her way.

I'm not anti-cop, not even close. I've been in situations where I looked to law enforcement for help and received it. When you put on a uniform, it makes you the "good guy." Some people rise to that responsibility and some abuse it. History continues to show that those who abuse it aren't held accountable, and when that happens, they deserve to be held up for all to see until there is justice.

Before starting at Peloton, I had scrubbed my Instagram of anything promoting or discussing or tagging Black Lives Matter, anything that I thought might make anyone uncomfortable. I didn't want people to find me on social media and judge me before they ever took my class. I didn't want them to have a preconceived notion of who I was and what I stood for—especially on such a large and generalized platform. Keeping my opinions on display on Instagram felt like showing them a menu before they'd even agreed to the dinner invitation. I wanted people to trust that I would have something to offer them, regardless of their established taste, so the images I left on Instagram were the most innocuous versions of me smiling and working out. The rest would follow soon enough.

Looking back, I don't know if scrubbing my account was the right thing to do, but I own it. But when the time came for me to speak, I did. And it meant something.

Six days after George Floyd was killed, I woke up from a restless sleep. I grabbed my phone to see what had gone on in the last eight hours, saw reports of the ongoing protests, and heard the drumbeat. I rolled out of my bed, sat on the floor next to it, hit record on my phone, and just started talking. "I wasn't going to say anything, because I didn't want to make you uncomfortable," I began. "I wasn't going to say anything because of how you might perceive me for it. It's easy to just toss me in the category of angry or mad Black woman. I'm mad but it's not because I'm a Black woman. I'm mad because I'm a human and what's happened, what's happening, what's continuing to happen, it's not human." I thought about my brothers, my nephews, the unjustifiable dangers they faced, and how urgent it was to keep them alive. "If having an uncomfortable conversation keeps my brothers alive," I continued, "if having an uncomfortable conversation keeps my nephews alive, then let's get uncomfortable. The first step is acknowledging the role that we all play in systemic racism." I remembered times I'd been in all-white spaces and felt like people were threatened by me. I said, "If you have fear when my brothers or someone who looks like my brothers passes you on the street, if you clench up, let's talk about it. Because talking about that fear keeps my nephews alive. Because acknowledging that fear, it keeps my brothers alive. If you're asking yourself what you can do, acknowledge those feelings. Talk with your children about those feelings. Get uncomfortable with those feelings. Feel those feelings. What happened on that tape, what we saw, it wasn't new. The only difference is this time they caught it on tape. Get uncomfortable. Don't allow the feelings to just rush past you. Feel them. Because that feeling keeps people that look like me safe. Acknowledging that feeling keeps people that look like me safe."

Only three months earlier, twenty-five-year-old Ahmaud Arbery had been shot as he jogged through the Georgia neighborhood where he grew up. How could this cycle end? I was here to witness it, so I had to help change it. "My nephews shouldn't fear going for a jog in his own neighborhood. If you're asking yourself what you can do, address your own feelings first. The feelings that we continue to pass down from generation to generation. If you're asking yourself what you can do, address those feelings with your children, so that we end the cycle, so that we don't continue to pass that fear that turns into hate down from generation to generation. If this makes you uncomfortable, good. Acknowledge it. Talk about it. Don't just move through it. Don't just scroll past it." Oh my god, how could I bring children into a world like this? Was I going to have to have the same talk with my kids that my parents had with my brothers? It may sound childish, but it just felt so unfair. "I just want my babies to live. I just want my babies to live freely, openly, just like yours. Freely and openly, just like yours. I just want them to live."

I posted the video to Instagram. I didn't know what

would happen. I had forty thousand followers. Maybe one or all of them would stop following me. But I thought about something Robin once said: "When you are yourself, your people are better able to find you." She was right. If you pretend to be someone else, people can't see you for who you are. When you speak your mind, it's like waving a flag people can see from a distance. Some will see it and say, "No, thanks, that's not for me," but I guarantee you the people in the back of the line, those people will see it and know to come.

By the next morning I had lost a few people, but I had gained about thirty thousand new followers. I had been scared to take action because I didn't want people to form opinions about me, but when I found the courage to speak without caring about what people thought, they hadn't run. They had connected. **When you show yourself as who you are, your people find you. Authenticity is the intersection of trust and truth.** I trusted that my truth was right. Anyone open-hearted would know that what I was saying was carried on the back of love. Far too often, we focus on what we might lose by being ourselves instead of seeing all that there is to be gained.

The next day, the medical examiner in Minnesota ruled George Floyd's death a homicide. It felt like the world was on fire—a devastating murder coming on top of a pandemic—and it was hard for all of us to work. How could I summon the bubbly, lighthearted energy needed to do my upcoming "pop" ride when *this* was happening? How was I supposed to be upbeat and inspirational when it felt like it was too hard to be either? I was grateful when an email came from the Peloton management team to the staff, alerting us to a call with our founder and CEO John Foley to discuss what we should do to promote an anti-racist vision in the company and the community.

Before the group call, my boss, Jen Cotter, the chief content officer of Peloton, called me to ask if I wanted to do a ride of solidarity to unite the members. Maybe I could say something that night in class. I didn't know exactly what I was committing to, but without hesitation I said yes.

The next day, I called John and asked if I had his blessing to speak my mind.

"Tunde," he said, "that's what you're here for. To be yourself." That validated my love for the company I worked for. People like Colin Kaepernick had lost their jobs for taking a stand. How lucky was I to work for a company where it was not only safe to speak my mind but encouraged? I was ready to speak out publicly, but I didn't know exactly how to do it from a bike.

On our group call, many plans were put forth that would lead to the Peloton Pledge—the company committed to investing $100 million over the next four years to fight racial injustice and inequity. It was a genuinely heartfelt discussion, and I felt proud to work for the company and hopeful that a difference could be made.

Someone on the group call suggested that we spread the word about my ride, to give people an opportunity to come with intention and solidarity. What started as a plan to simply have me comment became a plan for a whole ride centered around the issue. We talked about whether to call it a Black Lives Matter ride, but, again, I didn't want to announce the menu. The BLM supporters would see the ride promoted on social media and would definitely come, but what about everyone else? I didn't want to just preach to the choir. I wanted to invite a broader audience—the person whose husband was against BLM, but who hadn't made their mind up yet. Or the person who believed that Black lives do matter but couldn't have that conversation with their uncle. I wanted people who were uncomfortable. Because even I was uncomfortable. I didn't study racial inequity in school. I wasn't used to sharing my opinions on the matter. I taught a cycling class. But I believed what I wanted to do was good, and I knew that it should come from a place of love.

I called Kristy, Kim, Max, and Johnny (we'd since broken up, but were on good terms) to poll them about what to call the class. Later that evening, Johnny called me back. "Speak Up," he said.

"Oh my god," I said. Suddenly, our call was interrupted. "Hold on," I said, "Kim's on the other line."

When I picked up the call, Kim said, "Tunde, you have to call it 'Speak Up.'"

Speak Up. It made perfect sense and reminded me of a moment two years earlier at the Sweat Shoppe. I was sitting outside with Elizabeth, Carlos's niece, and we were catching up with each other's lives. We both had great things going on, and it was kind of a feel-good moment.

Then Elizabeth said, "Tunde, why is it that we as women only come together for one of two things: to talk about our partners or to gossip about other women? We don't always talk about ourselves, our hopes, our ambitions."

I made her repeat what she'd just said, and it sat with me for a week. Was this true? If it was, why didn't women spend more time building each other up? It was a good time in my life. I was tapping into a newfound joy. Every time I taught, I felt the drumbeat of purpose driving me forward. I wanted to give people some of what I was feeling.

Becoming an instructor had happened for me because I told the right people about my dream. They didn't say, "But you have a great job, but you travel so much for work, but you don't have experience . . ." Instead, they said, "You can do this. You *should* do this." *What if I created an accountability circle for women?* I now thought. *We'll share our ambitions, and then hold each other accountable to achieve them, just like my friends held me accountable.* I wanted women to be able to speak, and that's what I called the group. SPEAK.

My friends were right. I had to call the ride Speak Up. I started to think about what I would say. Peloton is loved by all different people all over the world—there were more than two and a half million members at the time—and lots of Black people worked with me there. I wanted to give them a platform, to bring some of those behind-the-scenes people into our community's homes. These weren't random stories. These were stories from people who contributed to the experience that the rider was having—people helping to bring them joy.

Later, at home, I listened to hours of music, looking for the perfect songs to help tell the story. At three in the morning, I finally got in bed to try to sleep, but my eyes were wide open and my mind was racing. I grabbed a pen and started writing. Not thinking, just letting the words come out. I didn't sleep until almost two days later. My brain wouldn't turn off. Every time I tried, I would pop back up. I didn't eat. I wasn't hungry. I wasn't tired. I felt energized, like I was supposed to be there in that moment.

Again, **I believe in living a life on purpose, of purpose, and with purpose.** As humans we're all here to support each other. To be of service to each other. Our purpose comes naturally to us. It's the thing we feel we're meant to do. My thoughts, I realized, mattered. Instead of shutting them out for being too painful or uncomfortable or controversial, I wrote down everything I was thinking. I felt a sense of certainty and alignment.

The night before the ride, I finally crashed. When I woke up the next morning, I had the most profound meditation of my life. I felt intensely aware that everything was happening as it should. *This morning is for me,* I told myself. *Today is my day. Any obstacle that arises is supposed to happen. I welcome it. Whatever happens is happening in my favor.* It was an expansion of the prayer my mother used to say, that whatever I said would be the right thing. If conflict came, I would be grateful for it. I felt like her prayer had been realized. And I was ready for it.

It was like I was having an out-of-body experience. I wasn't nervous. I had butterflies, but I was in control of my energy. As I arrived at work, I spoke calmly. I moved calmly. I was so aware of everything. I felt like I was supposed to be there on that day. Everything that was happening was part of it. I walked into the empty studio wearing my mask, and then went into a dressing room by myself. I played some music, and then I called my friend Erica. When I said, "Hi," she answered, "Mmm-hmm," as if she'd been expecting my call.

"Tunde, this is easy."

I knew what she meant. Erica thinks that when you're supposed to be doing something, it's easy. And telling yourself that takes the pressure off. It's true. People would either understand what I was trying to communicate, or they would somehow misconstrue my words. That was out of my hands. I wanted them to know I was coming from a place of love and compassion and hoped they would not judge but listen. I wasn't an expert at the issue, but, as I had learned, my experience alone made me worthy to speak. My opinions weren't the only opinions, but they were worth hearing.

One thing was for sure, though: I wasn't going to hold back. I had always designed my rides to be as inclusive as possible, to welcome everybody, but it was okay if this ride made some people uncomfortable. People need to be uncomfortable to change.

It was somber in the studio that day, particularly for the Black and brown staff on the schedule. They looked like they were in mourning, but also had the slow, simmering energy of an uprising. We were all drained, but emboldened. Empowered. I went through my intro, testing the mic, and I looked over at Ivan, the studio staff manager. He looked at me, and the expression on his face was how you'd look at someone when you know they're going off to lead a battle. His face said, "You've got this."

I got on the bike. I wore all black because the moment was important and grave. They cued me to start.

"We protect ourselves from knowing the pain of others," I began, "because it's painful and it's uncomfortable. It floods our senses when it's faced head-on and we become overwhelmed with it. In order to be woke, in order to wake up, we must be willing to lean into it. We must be willing to lean into the discomfort. The purpose over the next thirty minutes is to lean into it, to learn from it, to change, and to grow. Ultimately, from there, we speak up."

The pain of others. That's what I wanted them to care about. That's what I wanted them to understand. That, I had decided in my intense three-day preparation, was what would inspire them to change and to fight for larger change. Empathy. My friend Aditi Shah wrote: "In many of the Eastern philosophies behind yoga and meditation practices, there is an understanding that each of our personal, individual liberation is deeply connected with collective liberation. We are all interconnected. We can see that with the spread of the pandemic. So, as interconnected beings—really, this movement is all of our responsibility."

The first song I played was J. Cole's "Trouble." In the

background, the choir sings, "Troubles of this world." I explained to those riding with me that usually I use the music to distract from the physical discomfort, to take away the pain. But I had chosen this song, and all of the songs on the playlist, to expose the pain, to inflict it, so we could all sit in it together.

"Because on the other side of pain is growth. Black lives matter. They've always mattered. This is not the first death this year, nor was it the first death this May. Black lives matter. They always mattered. The question is why did it take this long to figure that out?" While I spoke, I cued everyone to work out, to increase resistance, to hit a certain cadence, trying to push them physically at the same time as I hoped to push them mentally and emotionally.

During the second song, Nina Simone's "Feeling Good," I glanced down at the leaderboard to see how many people were there. I usually had three or four thousand people at my live rides. But today there were twenty-two thousand. Twenty-two thousand people, riding with me, who had showed up to hear what I had to say.

"Every class, I say 'season to taste.' I provide ingredients, and then you cook what you want with those ingredients. I didn't start today's class like that. Today, we eat what I want. Today, we eat what I put on the menu. If you don't like it, you spit it up, but first, we try. First, we try it."

Throughout the ride, I shared some of what the other Peloton instructors had told me about what George Floyd meant to us, and what had happened to Breonna Taylor, and to Ahmaud Arbery, and to the long list of other names that had come before them, and the long list of names there likely would be after them if we didn't step up. I told them that Shakah Thomas, a Black thirty-one-year-old Peloton senior production tech, had told me, "We don't just hurt in times like this. We don't pause our hurt and our pain until the next George Floyd situation. Black people, we hurt in the in-between."

I told them what Asia Poole, a Black female associate producer, age twenty-six, said: "You acknowledge acts of hate and injustice when I'm in the room. I ask that you do the same when I'm not in the room."

I shared with them how it felt to be Xavier Green, a twenty-eight-year-old Black man who worked in the Peloton copyright department: "It's been building up for a while. The subconscious trauma that's now made its head. The fear of my gut every time I hear a police siren. The subconscious decision to remove my hoodie when I'm in an all-white space. The way my voice changes when I'm in an all-white space. It's heavy on my back, on my conscious, on my soul."

Halfway through, I felt like I was in a wildly deep, raw, emotional, unapologetic space. I was in pain. I was saying heavy things. I had an important message that I wanted to deliver, so I'd written a lot out of what I wanted to say, but once I started talking, I went off-script. There were moments where I wasn't thinking—the words just came over me and out of me. I was a vessel. *Was I going too hard?*

I didn't know if people wanted to hear it, if they would like or hate what I was trying to say. Were they logging out? Maybe everyone had left the ride. Even if six thousand stayed to listen, that would be a win, I told myself. I glanced down at the leaderboard and saw the numbers. All twenty-two thousand people were still there with me. Months earlier, I was scared to speak my truth or keep it posted for all to see on Instagram. Now a full stadium's worth of people were there, listening to what I had to say. We were in this together. Then I knew that what I was doing was right. I knew to keep speaking my mind.

"All lives matter. This is all lives. If Black lives don't matter, then all lives can't matter. We just want to be a part of the *all*. All lives matter. **If Black lives don't matter, there is no all.** We have to be willing to lean into the discomfort. We protect ourselves from knowing the pain of others, because it's painful and it's uncomfortable. It floods our senses until it overwhelms us. But if we want to wake up, we have to be willing to lean into it. From there, we evoke learning, growth, change, and then ultimately, we're given the power, the freedom to find our voice, to speak up. Black lives matter, but they've always mattered. What took us so long?"

As we approached the final songs, I wanted to end with hope. When I was a kid, I went to two churches on Sunday. The first was the all-white church down the street from my house. I lived in a predominantly white neighborhood in Houston, and my best friend was my neighbor Beth. We did everything together, including going to the church where her dad was the pastor, and her mom was the head of the choir. It was a big church, maybe eight hundred people, and I was the only Black person. I sang in the choir—songs like "Holy, Holy, Holy" and "Go Tell It on the Mountain." Everyone was kind to me, but I knew I looked different. I felt alien, but still welcomed.

After that service, my parents would pick me up and take me to the African church. I was in the choir at this church, too, and we sang the same songs, but differently. In the white church, everyone was quiet and still during the sermon. In the African church, people were dancing and singing and calling out "amen" and "hallelujah" whenever they felt compelled. (It was "ah-men" in the white church and "a-men" in the African church.) At the white church they'd never had a congregant named Tunde. At the African church, I didn't stick out. Everyone looked like me, and there was even a guy who shared my name, which is common in Nigeria, like being an Emily or a Michael. After white church, we were served donuts, which I loved, and at African church we were served a full meal with rice and meats. White church was only an hour; African church was three hours long, and we'd eat there—then also go to lunch afterward with assorted aunties and uncles and cousins from our sprawling Nigerian community (we ate a lot).

I liked both churches and didn't mind changing the way I sat, listened, talked, moved, and ate when I went from one to the other. It was clear to me that everyone just loved God. Everyone wanted to find joy together.

Everyone believed that we were there for a purpose and that it was good. We were all the same, we just went about it differently. And I felt like the two churches taught me to be a bridge between cultures, between people and ideas.

My whole life has taught me to see color, and straddling two cultures only made me more curious and accepting. Rather than judging or hating each other for our differences, it's beautiful to come together to celebrate and learn from each other. Because of my upbringing, I acknowledge and accept and love that.

I didn't give the Speak Up riders a cool-down, because I wanted them to stay in the feeling. I didn't want it to end or diminish. And when it did, I wanted them to come back to a feeling of hope.

"I'm tired, but I can't let my tired supersede hope," I said as we started to slow down. "Martin Luther King Jr. was tired. If he had allowed tired to supersede hope, he wouldn't have led the march in Selma that day. I'm tired, yeah, but I'm more hopeful than I am tired. This time feels different. Let your hope supersede your tired."

The song "Peace Train" was playing, and I quoted it. I could feel its message about hope—that one day the world would be as one—resonating with the people I couldn't see.

"Peloton, go out and create great change."

I closed the ride out with a quote from Martin Luther King Jr.: "Darkness cannot drive out darkness, only light can do that. Hate cannot drive out hate, only love can do that." The ride ended, and I unclipped. Chelsea Jackson Roberts was leading a Breathe In, Speak Up meditation to follow the ride. She was in the studio next door, and I got out my phone to sign in to her class. I never lie down on the podium—why would I? It's sweaty and nasty—but I lay down and closed my eyes to listen. My heart rate was falling, and I was still coming down off the ride, not knowing what to feel about what I'd just done. Everything had happened so fast that I was trying to get the rest of me to catch up to what had just come out of me.

When Chelsea was finished, I opened my eyes and looked up and saw a blue light from one of the cameras, flashing at me. I felt my body elevated on the podium. There it was. My life had finally synced up to the vision I'd had some three years before. I'd known that I would be cycling for the rest of my life, that I'd be teaching it, and that I'd be teaching it on the world's biggest platform. What I'd seen in that premonition, I'd met in this hour. At the time, that Speak Up ride was the second-highest-attended live class Peloton had ever had. I was teaching, and it was more than just cycling. I started laughing, then crying.

I walked out of the studio and Ivan and KJ and the other techs were there, crying. We weren't supposed to touch because of the pandemic, but KJ and Ivan hugged me. Outside the studio, Jess Sims was waiting for me. I looked at her to see what she thought, but she just handed me her phone. She had screen-recorded a moment of the ride. I watched and saw myself quoting MLK: *Power is the ability to effect change. I can't sugarcoat my words, because if I sugarcoat my words, they'll lose their power.* I couldn't believe the woman I was watching was me. There was so much power coming out of my voice. Power, but not anger. Power and love. I sounded like a leader, like the people I'd seen at rallies and marches, and at church. With the phone still in my hand, I dropped to my knees and covered my mouth.

"I hope you're so proud of yourself," Jess told me.

All I could say was, "Wow, wow, wow."

Not long after that, a writer from the *New York Times* reached out, wanting to interview me about the Speak Up ride. I truly felt the universe was telling me that it was the right time to fully reveal who I was and what I believed, the right time to lean into the discomfort of expressing myself. I didn't have to be universally acceptable. I just had to speak up.

And it worked.

Thousands of people reached out to me on social media. Black people felt seen and heard by the Peloton community. White people felt empathetic and empowered. Everyone was talking about what they could do, what they should do.

"My wife made me take the ride," one man messaged me to say. "I was on the 'other side.' I found the term Black Lives Matter offensive because all lives matter. But after that ride I get it. I stand with you." He had heard me when I said, "If Black lives don't matter, there is no all."

Another person wrote to say that she had never ridden

with me because I look so different from her. She'd scrolled past my face hundreds of times. "I didn't think we'd have anything in common because we have different backgrounds," she wrote, which was hurtful to have confirmed, to hear that people would judge me based on the color of my skin—if someone wouldn't invest twenty minutes in me because we looked different, where else in life were they, perhaps unconsciously, unwilling to invest in someone who doesn't look like them? Would they hire someone who looked like me, investing years in a Black employee when they wouldn't take a twenty-minute class? Would they trust a Black friend? Mentor a Black youth? But she didn't just DM it to me privately. She also posted it to her feed, admitting it to everyone. She was ready to speak up so other people would admit their own biases. It still stung, but I realized and understood that I had to let her bravery be bigger than my feelings. She was seeing things in new ways, and now that she saw it, she couldn't unsee it. As other people told me after the ride, the pain of saying nothing was worse than the pain of saying the wrong thing. That is how we get to real change, by facing the stuff that hurts to admit. I wanted people to be able to speak their truth safely and listen safely.

After the ride, I wanted to keep the conversation going. After all, this is human behavior. We all participate—on the subway we choose a seat next to someone who looks like us. In an elevator we strike up conversation with someone who feels familiar. Systemic racism and bias are real. It wasn't about one ride, or about checking off a diversity box. It was about feeling it. The more of us who had the audacity to face our prejudices, to be that vulnerable, the more apt we would be to create the change we need to. We all needed to listen. Not just to hear. But to feel. People were so concerned with saying the right thing, they were missing that when you listen to feel, the pain of saying nothing is worse than the pain of saying the wrong thing.

I'd always known that I wanted to bring SPEAK to life in a more consistent way, so I launched an interview series on Instagram, showcasing the voices of Black celebrities so that people could see that even they had dealt with racism.

I talked to Venus Williams about winning Wimbledon for the first time at age nineteen and using her power to advocate for equal prize money for men and women. I talked to Scott Evans about how, when we pursue our dreams, we should accept that we're going to fail along the way. I talked to Cynthia Erivo about being a Black opera singer, and how the stories in her genre have been written without people of color. And to Ryan Michelle Bathe, who told me, "You can't lead without empathy. You can be in power without empathy, but I don't know that you can be a true leader. I don't think that you can truly hear the concerns of people and then metabolize that in actual items without being able to metabolize people's fears and hurts and hopes and dreams." Jess Sims, my fellow Peloton instructor, talked about being biracial and how offensive it was when people told her she was "the prettiest Black woman" they'd ever seen.

I discovered that this was what I wanted to do. To speak to anybody who would listen. Having a job where I could say what I thought was a privilege, and my work happened to bring me in front of thousands of people. I wanted to use that as best I could.

My following kept growing; I'd be walking my dog, and people would greet him with "Hey, Cesar!" or stop and say hi. Being recognized is a novelty, but now it had a purpose, and it was a privilege. People approached me to share that they'd taken the ride and been impacted—changed, even. It's one thing to teach to a silent room, to say things and hope they mean something, but to actually meet the people on the other side of the screen who saw me at my most vulnerable and listened was so rewarding. I wasn't an actor, and when I put myself in front of people, I exposed myself to them in the most authentic way I knew. The more authentic I was, the more I connected with people. I grew up thinking I wasn't skinny enough. I didn't finish college and felt like I wasn't educated enough. And yet I was invited to speak at Howard, and then at Princeton. When you show yourself as you are, people recognize you. Your people flock to you.

When history reveals itself, we will all either say we watched the world as it was being created or we had a hand in its creation. We can't speak only to people who look like us, to people who are like-minded. If we do that, then we're speaking to ourselves. To create change we have to broaden our minds and our reach and our voices. Let's do it together.

My goal for myself, for you, for all of us, is to go out and create, to go out and demand change. When they write books about this moment in time, I want to say I had a hand in the change.

Look what came from me using my voice and my platform for good. I was able to speak to people who might not have invited my message into their space, who might not know Black people or might not live near any. I had unique access to these people, and they have access to other people. And some number of those people will become part of the movement and reach out to other people. You don't need to reach twenty-two thousand people. Maybe your job is to access one. Maybe that's where you create change. Who knows how far it will lead?

TEN

The Chop

My friend Billie's response to the Speak Up ride was to tell me to cut off all my hair. This wasn't as random as it might sound: she had known that cutting off all my hair was something I'd always wanted to do. "You were so vulnerable in that ride," she said. "You brought your full self to this moment. The next step is to show up fully *for* yourself."

Here's something you should know about Black hair: It's not just hair. It's political, it's practical, it's personal. It's intentional. Yes, braids are cute and stylish, but they also protect your hair from breaking. And yet, they (and a lot of other styles) prompt strong reactions. A lot of Black women have been told they can't come to work with braids because it's not professional-looking. This is a workplace battle that Black women have fought and will continue to fight. Being told you can't wear your hair in braids is not like being told you can't wear jeans to the office. It's singling someone out. It's rejecting identity. Imagine someone telling you that you can't wear the hairstyle that your ancestors have been wearing since the dawn of time to protect their hair—and that you need to style it to look more like theirs. It's an everyday indignation, so whenever we have the chance to express ourselves through our hair, it's important to us to seize it.

I had always been fascinated with short hair, even though I'd worn a weave, extensions, or braids every day since I was in elementary school. The first time I wore a fake ponytail was in kindergarten. My hair was coarse and didn't swing back and forth like the other girls in my class, who were all white. I begged my mother to let me wear a ponytail, and she finally agreed to put one on me, though she warned me it might cause some trouble. I bounced into kindergarten the next day, with my hair bouncing along with me. It felt amazing—until Miss Green called on me in front of the class. "Tunde!" I looked up to see that she was holding my ponytail in her hand. It must have fallen off. All the kids laughed. "Let me put it back on for you," Miss Green said gently. I walked to the front of the classroom and stood while she tried to figure out how to reattach it. I was mortified. When I came home, I was furious at my mother.

"This is why I said you couldn't wear it!" she reminded me.

Only a couple of years after that, I started wearing braids all the time. My mother had always said my hair had to be under her rules while I was young—"When you're old enough that people know you're getting your own self ready, you can do whatever you want. But while people think it's me, you have to look put together."—and though it took nine to ten hours to braid my hair, I loved sitting between my mother's knees while she did it. We'd stay up all night together to get it done, and that was a time when we talked about anything and everything.

At first I just thought I looked cute, but then I started depending on the braids to feel confident. I kept them, even when they limited me. I could never get my hair wet. The braids—my attachment to them—are why I never learned to swim. As I got older, I relied on my hair the same way I relied on makeup to make me feel good about myself. I wasn't comfortable being seen as myself. I had to have my armor on.

And yet, I always fantasized about cutting my hair. The women I saw with short hair struck me as confident and strong. Most of the time my mom wore wigs or braids— my brothers liked it curly and bouncy, like Oprah's—but I thought she was the most beautiful in the rare times when her hair was short. I could see her whole face, her laugh, her strength. Because of that, I felt more connected to her soul. As a makeup artist, I became hyperaware of the bone structure in people's faces and appreciated how it was highlighted by short hair. I also thought it said to the world, *I don't need my hair to be feminine. I don't need a certain hairstyle to be beautiful. I'm enough.*

Of all the messages society sends us about our bodies,

hair—our manes!—get the lion's share of the attention. We have good hair days and bad hair days. We hide behind it. We rely on it for glamour and femininity. When I started thinking about cutting off my hair, I wasn't confident enough to do it. "When I'm thirty-five I'll be old and married," I said to myself. "I'll be confident enough to do it then." In the intervening years, I'd never stopped thinking about it. I liked the way Black women could change it up—I liked wearing braids, extensions, and playing with my look. But I saw that people reacted to me differently when my hair changed. If I had a long, silky, straight weave, I got catcalls from Black men and more attention from white and Latino men. If I wore dreads, they said, "Hey, sister" or "Hey, queen" with respect in their voices. I kept my hair out of braids for five months or so when I started at Peloton because I thought people would think I was too Black, too tough, and too mean. What would they say if I was bare-headed, my whole face speaking for me? Would it make me more confident? Would it make me less attractive? Who would I be?

My niece and I are very close. Since my mother passed away, I have always made it a priority to spend time alone with her. She has a Black father and a white mother, and beautiful, big, curly hair—but she wets and mousses it to make it lie flat. She hates her curls. I always tell her that her hair is beautiful in its natural form, but she just wants to look like everyone else around her. She also has recently blossomed into a curvy young girl, with a waist/hip differential that I, as someone with a square body, have always envied. When I visit her, we like to do at-home spa days, and one day, I left her bedroom so she could change in private. I realized I had to go back in to grab something, and when I did, my niece immediately hid herself behind a towel. That was my first clue that her feelings about her body were growing more complicated. We had a family picture day scheduled the next day, and all of us planned to wear white. I had brought a backup dress for her, so she tried it on after she showered. She looked beautiful, but I could see that she was pouting.

"I hate these hip thingies," she announced. "I don't understand why my body sticks out like this and yours goes straight down." I was shocked, and sad. I would have killed to have the body of this eleven-year-old girl! It pained me to see her look in the mirror at such a young age and already have a formed opinion that what she had was not enough, too much, or wrong. But I could see that she'd internalized the message we all get: what is right is what other people have, and what is wrong is what we were born with. We look at other people's bodies and lives with envy. Why don't we like our own selves best? It was so clear to me that she was beautiful just as she was. We collect insecurities throughout our lives, without paying attention to who is telling us we are too much or not enough. Their voices become the voice in our own heads, spinning in a loop of self-criticism, and every time we listen to them, we give them power. You are what you think you are, so you have to be mindful of what you think.

In middle school, a Black kid named A.J. came up to me one day and told me that his friend Duane liked me. For a moment, I felt a flutter of excitement. Not that I had any particular feelings for Duane, but I wanted to be noticed. I wanted to be liked by a boy—any boy! But then A.J. said, "He thinks you're cute for a dark-skinned girl, but he'll never date you because you're too dark." *Too dark*. There were other Black kids in my school, but Duane happened to be the only other kid who was as dark as I was.

"He's ugly. I don't like him anyway," I retorted. I felt hurt and embarrassed, but I played it cool. There were two or three more periods of school left, and I didn't want people to see me cry. The bell couldn't ring fast enough. On the school bus home, I sat by myself, looking out the window. I took shallow breaths, knowing if I inhaled any more air, tears would roll down my face. I felt like the big, Black, and dark-skinned girl I was, surrounded by skinny, white, pretty girls. All I wanted was to fit in, but I felt like an other.

I got off the school bus, and the second I walked into our house, I burst into tears. Why did I have to be in this dark skin? Was this why no boys liked me? Duane was dark, but it was okay for him because he was a boy. My brother Tony was playing video games in the living room. "I hate my skin," I said to him. "It's too dark. How do I get my skin lighter?"

"Soak it in bleach," he said casually, and went back to his video game.

For the record, I'm fairly confident that Tony wasn't trying to kill me. He must have heard some mention of skin-bleaching creams and assumed regular bleach would do the trick. It sounded like the right answer at the time, so I walked into the laundry room and grabbed a bottle of bleach, filled the bathtub with scalding water, and poured a good amount of it in. The odor was intense, like a swimming pool times 100. I wrinkled my nose as I prepared to dunk myself in the tub. I didn't want to smell like bleach. I decided to do a test on my hand by pouring straight bleach into a bowl and sticking my hand in it. I waited for what felt like a long time, watching my hand closely for any changes. When I pulled my hand out, it wasn't any lighter. So I rinsed the bleach off my hand and drained the tub. I was disappointed that it didn't work and resigned to living with and in this skin for the rest of my life. There was no way out.

I didn't hate my dark skin, and I didn't think about it every day, but my feelings about it were unresolved until a year or so later when I was sitting cross-legged in the living room, watching TV, and a Black woman came onto the screen. She was stunning. The most beautiful woman I'd seen in my life, and she was dark, just like me. I screamed to my mother, who was in the kitchen making dinner. She hurried into the living room. "What's wrong?"

"Look," I said. "She's beautiful."

"Yeah," my mom said, not catching my point.

"And she has dark skin," I said.

"Yeah, she has dark skin," my mother said. My mother's

skin was significantly lighter than mine. I got my dark skin from my father's side. My siblings were dark, too, but I was the darkest. I don't think she had any idea that I worried about how dark I was until that moment.

"Does that mean I can have dark skin and be beautiful, too?"

I can only imagine what my mother thought. She was probably at a loss—she had always told me I was beautiful because I shined, and I doubt she could imagine what would bring me to think otherwise. "Of course," my mother said. "Don't you know how beautiful you are?"

The woman I saw on the screen that day with my mother was Naomi Campbell, and many years later I would see her at a fashion show and finally have a chance to thank her for showing a little girl that any color could be beautiful.

The world still told me I was different. *You're beautiful for a Black girl* would become a phrase I heard way too many times. *She's pretty, but she's so dark-skinned*—another phrase I've heard whispered far too often. The color of my skin isn't the same as the skin of the people who say these things: my Black skin is illuminated by the sun and it beams in the dark. My Black skin does not shift, and it does not alter. My Black skin is my essence, and it makes me myself.

These days, Black women DM me to send me pictures of their daughters watching me on the screen as they bike. Often the mom has lighter skin than her daughter, and she writes something along the lines of: "It means so much to her to see you." This is how representation reverberates in our lives, and it's a two-way street. That mother is giving back to me. Beauty is a continuous circle. It starts inward, pushes outward, and then loops back in. Self-love follows the same route, starting on the inside and later becoming visible on the outside, and people respond to it. Once we are able to foster our inner beauty, we are able to push it outward and pull it right back in, and the circle continues. In short, love yourself. The world will recognize it and send that love right back to you.

Too muscular. Too thin. Too dark. Too light. Too tall. Too short. Too outspoken. Too quiet. We are so quick to put people in boxes, where we think they belong. We don't need to let other people set the standard for how we want to live. When I see my muscles, I think about how they serve me. I can lift more weight. When it comes to carrying groceries, I'm a one-trip wonder. When I travel, I don't think twice about putting luggage in the over-head compartment. These arms are a gift, and I've learned to appreciate them on my own terms. I pride myself on looking different. I pride myself on being different.

It took me a whole year after the Speak Up ride to get my courage up for the big chop. After all these years of waiting to be thirty-five, settled, in a life where cutting off my hair couldn't possibly matter to anyone, it was ironic that I found myself on a public platform for the first time in my life. Making a big change felt so much scarier and riskier now that more people knew who I was.

There were so many people out there standing ready to judge me. But my position also gave me increased power. Shaving my head was something I could do—and wanted to do—for myself. I wanted to prove to myself that I was pretty without extensions. I wanted to prove that hair was nothing more than an accessory to me. I wanted to prove that I could handle whatever people thought of me. Now I was thirty-five. I had shown up as my whole self. Wasn't now the time to cut away the extra, the limiting beliefs, the fear of being seen as too anything? I was prepared to step into it.

I messaged an Instagram makeup artist I follow who has short, buzzed hair, asking for advice. She recommended Larry the Barber. A lot of what he posted on Instagram were big chops—women letting go of masses of hair—which immediately appealed to me. I wanted someone who understood the emotional component for the woman sitting in a chair and getting her hair cut off. I made an appointment for a month away, to give myself time to decide, and make sure it felt right. For four weeks, I stayed up every night, sending pictures of potential cuts to my friends, squinting my eyes, and trying to picture myself with no hair. Then, one day, I just wanted to hurry and get it done. I changed my appointment to the earliest one available.

My ex-boyfriend Johnny was in town, and I decided to bring him and my friend Sam with me for the chop. To be honest, I was curious to find out whether Johnny would still think I was beautiful with my natural hair.

Some guys I dated here and there never got to see my natural hair. But when I'd taken my braids out for a day or two in between getting new ones, Johnny had complimented me more than usual. When someone gives you a compliment and you don't have makeup on, it feels different. You know it's you and not the idealized image you've constructed. He liked me in my natural state, and I felt seen by him.

We took a train to deep Brooklyn to see Larry. It was an hour-long train ride, and the whole time I still wasn't sure I'd go through with it; I figured I'd decide when I got there. We arrived, and I sat down in the chair. Larry was Caribbean, and island music filled the room. I took off my hat. I heard the sound of his clippers. I had thought he'd start on the side, by my ear, so I'd be able to see what my head looked like—that's a look on its own, the side shave—so if I got cold feet, I could stop him before he did the whole thing. But he surprised me by shaving right down the middle.

"Oh!" I said. "That's how we're going to start this?"

He laughed and smiled. "You have to bite the bullet. This is the only way to do it."

Johnny and Sam were beaming. I watched my hair fall onto my shoulders without reacting. Then Larry finished. I was surprised to realize that after all that buildup—years of it—I didn't feel emotional. My first thought was, *Okay, this is what my head looks like.* I was amazed that I'd gone through with it, and relieved that I didn't have a weird-shaped head.

"I thought it was impossible for you to be more beautiful," Johnny said, looking right at me, "but you are so beautiful!"

I felt the chill in the room and put on my hat for the subway home, still weirdly unemotional. But later that night, I looked at myself in the mirror and started crying. I couldn't believe I'd done it. It felt like I'd taken off a mask. My hair truly wasn't me. It didn't control how I thought of myself. After all these years of wearing the weave, it was freeing to show myself I could be exactly who I am.

For the next few days, I wore a wig when I left my apartment, wanting to form an opinion about my haircut for myself before the world told me how they felt about it. Then, one day, I showed up at the Peloton studio wearing a sideways cap with the wig. (I had been trying to bring back the sideways cap, without much success.) Jess King was in the dressing room next to mine. I knocked on her door, and when she answered, I pulled off the hat and the wig.

She gasped in surprise. "I can see you," she said. "For the first time I can see all of you."

Oh my god, did I think I was fooling everyone? I had cut my hair to be free, and Jess saw that immediately. I knew I was hiding behind that hair—but who else knew it, too?

I like change, and I'll change my hair again. I'm not against extensions. I love braids, and I'm excited for the day I'll wear them again. But what's more exciting is to know that the girl who's underneath it is still just as confident and beautiful and even more free. I now know where I stop, and the presentation begins. Jess King once asked me, "Why do we say 'dance like nobody's watching'? Shouldn't we be able to dance freely when everyone is watching?" She was right. When you are true to yourself, who cares who is watching? Why live freely only when there is no one to witness it? Where's the freedom in that? When we're not feeling confident, it comes back to trust. The voice in our head telling us to do something or not is real—we just need to trust it. Do it. Do it before you're ready. Face your challenges. Write your own narrative. Don't let your fear hold you hostage.

When I change my hair next time, it will be for myself, on my terms, not because I need the world to think I'm beautiful.

The day I unveiled myself to Jess, I led a ride for Women's History Month, wearing a bright-red outfit with my newly shaved head on display. I didn't bring up the chop until close to the end of class, because I felt the point was to celebrate women and their power, not me and mine, but at the end of the ride, I addressed the elephant in the room. I wanted to acknowledge coming into my own power with everyone who was on that ride with me.

"I am so proud of myself," I said. "I did something that I've always wanted to do. I put it off for so long. I was so worried about what everyone's opinion would be. I have muscles and I didn't want to lose my femininity. I didn't want people to judge me. People stereotype people based on how they look. But I wanted to do it, so I did it anyway. I'm proud of myself for letting everyone's opinion of me go."

Soon after that, on Instagram, one of my followers, Krys Burnette, posted my comments with a caption of her own: "When people ask me why I'm obsessed with Peloton, it's this. There is no experience, no commercial brand that has ever let Black women step into their power for the world to see authentically. Tunde is having a moment not just because she cut her hair but because she cut off the weight of every stereotype about Black women and their relationship to their sense of self and their sense of worth. Every Black woman watching this understands."

The same week I came out with my short hair, some of the people who took my ride let me know they were no longer leading with fear. For some of them, that meant cutting their hair like I did, or feeling free enough to wear it curly or down. For others, it meant leaving the house without makeup. Owning their freckles. Showing their curves. Being unapologetically loud. We were saying to the world, "See me as I am." That's incredibly freeing. I was receiving screenshots from friends who'd seen people on FB who'd cut their hair saying that I had inspired them. One day, I ran into a white woman on the street who had shaved hair like mine. "I love your hair," I told her.

She replied, "What you said in your ride actually inspired me to do it."

At the end of the day this is about more than just Black hair. It's about women making a choice to let go of what everyone thinks, of how we want to be seen, or how we're told we should be seen, or how we hope we'll be seen, and finally allowing ourselves to make decisions based on how we see ourselves and how we want to see ourselves. We decide how we want to show up for ourselves—and that's also allowed to change over time. Why shouldn't we experiment? Why shouldn't we take risks? Why shouldn't we be bold?

ELEVEN

Always There

Growing up, I was always a good girl. Compared to the other Nigerian parents I knew, mine were lenient, but compared to the parents of my American friends at school, they were strict. There was only one friend at whose house I was allowed to sleep over—Beth, our neighbor whose parents were our white church minister and choir director, and when I responded to my mom, it was never "yes," only "yes, ma'am."

When he was young, my oldest brother, Tony, got into a fair amount of trouble. I saw how much it upset my mother and, either because it was my nature or because I didn't like seeing her upset, or both, I was determined not to do the same. My parents made the rules, and I followed them (well, except for when I would sneak out to go to salsa clubs with friends, or hang out with the stoners without getting stoned). By the time I was out in LA, living on my own, rule-following was ingrained in me. I went out, I partied, but I was always reliable, and nurturing, too. The voice of reason, the one who got everyone to talk again. I got this from my mother. She always tried to get everyone to come together with love. If a friend or an aunt was struggling with her kids, her relationships, or her work, my mother was the first person they called. If others were fighting, she was the mediator.

It was just after Christmas 2011, nearly three years after we had lost my brother Tope, when Tony called to tell me that our dad had gone into the hospital. He hadn't been in good health lately—he'd had diabetes for a long time and didn't manage it in terms of food, exercise, and wellness. Now his kidney and liver were failing, and his leg had swollen up. I was working for a cosmetics company in Topanga under Jessica, the same boss I'd had when I lost my brother, and when I told her about my dad, she immediately instructed me to go home.

"No, he's okay," I said. "I'll go home if it gets bad."

"You're leaving tomorrow," she insisted.

I flew to Houston the next morning, and when I arrived I was told he was still in the hospital, but he was doing better, and they were talking about releasing him soon. My dad's mind was already on getting back to work. His whole identity revolved around being a provider, and his sickness didn't change that, despite the fact that his vision wasn't as good as it used to be, and it was clear to the rest of us that he wouldn't be able to work much longer. He had the relentless work ethic of an immigrant. Nothing would stop him. As a driver, he'd always been great at directions, but he had the idea that a GPS would help him now that he couldn't see the street signs as clearly. I had come to Houston with a late Christmas present for him, and I gave it to him in his hospital bed. It was the GPS he'd been longing for. He started crying. It was one of the few times I'd ever seen him cry. Here he was, getting fluid drained from his legs, and getting emotional over being able to return to work. My dad, whom I'd always taken for granted. I looked at him now and thought, *This man has had a hard life. What has he ever done for himself? And here he is in the hospital, still worrying about providing for his family.*

After two weeks, he was released from the hospital. I'd stayed in town, and went to all of his doctors' appointments. The liver specialist told him what to eat and what to avoid. Then the kidney doctor gave him a different set of restrictions, contradicting the liver guy. By the time we'd seen all the specialists, it felt like there was only one food that everyone agreed would be good for him to eat: water, with a side of air.

I wanted him to take good care of himself, so before I left I made a chart for him and my mother listing which foods were good for him and offering meal ideas. I told him exactly what he could order at Subway, and I tried to incorporate some authentic Nigerian food into the plan so he could still enjoy some of his favorites.

One evening, as I was working on the chart, he walked past me wearing his regular house uniform: Fruit of the

Loom white underwear and socks. Then, he looked me in the eye and said, "I know you're going to be the one to do everything." I knew exactly what he meant. When he passed, I would be the one to organize things, just as I was doing now. I would plan the funeral. I would manage the finances. I would make sure whatever needed to be done got done. He said it almost apologetically, like he knew it would all fall on me, but it was also a recognition of who I was, of the role I had in the family. It hurt to acknowledge that he was on limited time, but I nodded because I could see he wanted reassurance that I would take care of things.

Once he was doing better, I went home. One night a couple of weeks later, I was at a friend's house in LA for a small get-together. We were watching Lana Del Rey's music video for the song "Video Games," and I'd had too much to drink, so I passed out on the sofa. (Like I said, I partied but responsibly!) At two in the morning, my phone rang. Not quite remembering where I was, I fumbled around to pick it up. It was my oldest brother, Tony.

"Dad's not breathing," he told me. I could hear my mother screaming, chanting, and praying in the background.

"What?" I said, still groggy. "Tony, what's going on? What? What?"

"It's okay, Mom," I heard him saying to my mother. Then, back to me, he said, "He's not breathing. The ambulance is here. We're going to follow them to the hospital." He kept the connection open as he got my mother into the car, and I could hear him continuing to comfort her as he drove. I was fully awake now. "He's going to be okay. He's going to be okay." My brother has always been the tough guy, but I could hear tears and worry and congestion in his voice.

How could this be happening? I thought. It had only been three years since we lost Tope. I wanted to go to the bathroom, but my legs felt too heavy, as if they were made of rock. I must have been yelling "What? What? What?" because my friend's husband came rushing to my side, concern on his face.

"My dad, my dad, he's not breathing," I gasped. "I have to pee. I can't walk."

He put an arm around my shoulder and helped me to the bathroom. He and his wife sat me on the toilet. I sat there, still on the phone, trying to make sense of what my brother and mom were saying.

"We're at the hospital," Tony finally said. "We'll call you back when we know more."

While I waited, I thought about the last couple of times I'd recently spoken to my father. Whenever I called, I would ask what he was eating, and he would reply, "Subway." I was glad he was taking care of himself and following my chart, but then, a week later, my mother told me that she had opened the car door and found an orange soda can and two banana peels. These were his two obsessions, but he wasn't supposed to be eating either of them. I had been planning to call him and yell at him, but I didn't. I was glad I hadn't—otherwise, our last conversation would have been a fight.

I had spoken to my mother again just the night before. As we talked, I'd pictured her sitting in Tope's recliner, the chair she'd started sitting in after he passed away, painting her nails. She was always either doing that or making jewelry. I could hear the TV blasting and knew that my dad was probably sitting on the floor next to her in his underwear and white socks. We hadn't talked since I'd found out about the bananas and orange soda, but she had me on speaker, and when I heard him shuffling around, I said, "Let me talk to Daddy."

He knew I wanted to tell him off, and I heard him say, "No, no, no. I don't need to talk to her. She knows how much I love her."

I'd been stunned. My dad never said *I love you.* It was such a rarity that whenever he said it, we'd all start cheering and laughing: "He did it!" we'd joke. Hearing him say it now, in his indirect way, melted my anger away.

"All right, love you guys. Good night," I said. It was the last time I heard his voice.

(Later, my mom told me that he'd done something else out of the ordinary that night: every night at 7 p.m. my mother's church group gathered on a conference line for an evening prayer. Mom was always part of it, but that day my father got on the phone and said a prayer for everyone himself.)

I was still at my friend's house when Tony confirmed that he was gone. I was in no condition to drive myself home. My friends called Kim and Brian (we were still to-gether at that point), and they came to pick me up. I felt like I was in a nightmare. I flew back home the next day. A friend picked me up at the airport, and when we drove up to the house, we saw that there was no place to park—just as when Tope died, Mom's friends had shown up to give her love. Just as I did after losing Tope, I walked up to the palm tree. It hadn't changed much, but I'd just lost another family member. So much was different. I took a deep breath to prepare myself. I knew what I was walking into. This was a moment I knew I would remember the rest of my life. I took several more deep breaths. Then I went inside.

My mother was in the living room, in Tope's recliner. The rest of my family, including my Nigerian aunties and uncles, were there. They had lost a friend. My mother had lost her husband. I was his only daughter—a daddy's girl—who could always be found sitting on his lap. When Tope passed away, I hadn't shown my emotions. I'd steeled myself so as not to cry around my parents, because I felt like I needed to parent them through their suffering—but now I didn't feel the same impulse. I let myself be the child that I was. I squeezed into the recliner next to my mom, lay my head on her chest, and wept.

And then, when it was time, I clicked into action. I organized everything. The service, the sorting of finances, keeping the family together and on track, who was taking on what tasks, and how we could best honor him. Re-membering what my father had said to me, I felt proud that he knew I'd be the one to step up. And this time, in spite of my grief, I felt a sense of comfort in knowing how to approach it. I'd been here before, in the shock of losing my little brother. I assumed I'd watch him grow up, get married, have children, but I had always known the day would come when I would have to say goodbye to my father. I was in immense pain, but I knew I would one day find peace.

As I was planning, I listened to Beyoncé's song "I Was Here" on repeat. The song served as a reminder that he was still here, an acknowledgment of the mark he had made in this world. In his children's lives. That, to me, was the beginning of healing, and I wanted to share it with my family and all his friends.

At his funeral, I told the congregation that the day before I'd gone to the Kroger's pharmacy to pick up my mom's medication. At the window, I'd said, "I'm picking up for Oyeneyin."

The pharmacist typed in my last name, then looked at me and said, "Festus!"

"I'm Festus's daughter," I said.

He laughed. "How's Festus?" he asked. "We haven't seen him."

"I'm sorry to have to tell you this, but he passed away a couple days ago."

A look of shock crossed his face, then he called someone from the back. "This is Festus's daughter," he told her when she came out to meet us.

She smiled at me. "How's Festus?" she asked. And then

he told her. They were both so emotional. I thanked them for their kindness and left to pick up another prescription at another pharmacy. When I gave my last name there, the same thing happened. And again at the dry cleaner. My father had passed all these people in his daily life and put his whole heart into these small interactions. How many people can say that when they pass, the people at the dry cleaner care? Dad didn't go out much, but he made an impact everywhere he went when he did. His time was never so precious that he missed being in the moment with the person in front of him. He made people laugh. He made them feel good. He'd tell the cashier at the grocery store that he liked her nail polish, just to show her he saw her as a fellow human. He had such an effect on everyone he came in contact with. I got that from him—curiosity about the people I encounter and an eagerness to connect. When we engage with the world around us, we don't just elevate our own awareness, we remind other people that they matter. This small but intentional gesture reverberates. When people feel like they matter, they pass that on, and so we buoy each other, tied together and keeping each other afloat in stormy seas.

I continued, explaining some more ways his legacy would live on: how Tony always had another idea for a business, an entrepreneurial and work spirit he'd inherited from Dad. Tosin was the entertainer. Like my father, everyone was always gathered around him, laughing.

My mother sat in the front row of the funeral parlor, and when I saw her face, I could tell that she knew my father would be proud. She had recognized my light at a young age, far before I did. But in that moment, she saw that I'd stepped into my own power and my gift.

"You just did him so well," she told me after the service. "Thank you for that." She was glad that I'd been able to do what she couldn't in that moment. To deliver that message, to share with all those people who my dad was, to connect in a way that I wasn't sure I could.

What makes me rise? The knowledge that I can. I've always been someone who steps up when most people step down. In high-pressure moments, I feel the thump of my heartbeat. It starts in the same place as fear—and that feeling used to scare me—but now when it happens I recognize it. I know that that feeling is what eventually carries me into confidence. My drumbeat, that swift and sure internal pulse, makes me feel alive and connected to my being and to the universe. It allows me to step into my losses to feel the power of understanding that I was built to handle this. I was the one who was supposed to do this.

I truly believe that everyone has this capacity, and that the more we can lean into it, the more it evolves to the next level. Sure, at first it might feel like anxiety. We might resist. It's human nature to want to shut down. But if you can surrender in those moments, that's when growth happens. You learn the most in moments of conflict. Your character emerges, and if you take notice, you can find yourself. That's the beauty of walking closer to that drumbeat. **The pain you experience today reveals itself as strength for tomorrow.** It comes back to what Sam Yo said about life repeating itself, and if we're aware when a situation comes around again, then we have the opportunity to take the next step forward.

After my dad passed away, my mom didn't go back to work. For two years she stayed in our house while Tony supported her. Because Houston was part of my territory for work, I was able to visit her every three months, but on one visit, I noticed that she had put on weight and kept complaining about stomach pain. She usually drove me to the airport, but this time she let my friend Callye drive me instead. Every time I said goodbye we both felt so sad. This time, as the car pulled away, she waved at me, and I could see that she was trying to be strong, trying not to cry. When she thought I was out of view, she lost it. Something was different. I started crying because I suspected that she was sicker than she was letting me know. She was afraid she would never see me again.

It wasn't the last time I saw her, but after I left, she got sicker. She moved in with Tony, who became her nurse. I felt guilty. Should I move home? Why was I in LA, in a job I was starting to question, when my mother was in Houston, dying?

My friend Max was a makeup artist, but he has always loved photography. We were doing a photo shoot, just for fun, when Tony called and said, "Mom is sick."

"Do I need to come home?" I asked.

"Not yet," he said.

Soon after, she and I talked. She'd been in and out of the hospital over the last year, but never overnight, so I was concerned. Tony had checked her in that morning, but she sounded fine. Two hours later, he called again. He told me that in order to change her bedding, the nurses had flipped my mom over, and she'd been going downhill ever since. I had to come home right away.

The entire plane ride I thought, *Please let me get there in time to say goodbye.* When I landed, I turned my phone on and called Tony to see if she was still here. I made it to the hospital, and she was still alive, but she was heavily medicated and not really coherent. Then, she had a moment of lucidity. "What are you doing here?" she demanded angrily. She was realizing, I knew, how serious it must be for me to miss work.

Two days after I arrived, Kim and Kristy joined me in Houston. We all stayed in the hospital, keeping vigil, barely sleeping. It was a heavy time and place, but it was also a moment of sisterhood. They were there with me, as they'd been with me when Tope died. They were always there when I needed them.

Whenever the haze of the morphine subsided, my mom insisted that she wanted to go home. Everyone in the family was arguing about whether she should be put on hospice care, while most of her friends still didn't know how sick she really was. She was a very private person— nineteen years earlier, she had been given a breast cancer diagnosis with three years to live and hadn't said a word.

Her biggest fear had been that Tope, who was only six years old at the time, wouldn't remember her. She'd been in remission ever since, but now it turned out she had a very aggressive ovarian cancer. Everyone around her saw this as a new battle without realizing how long she'd quietly been living on borrowed time.

Ultimately, we brought Mom to Tony's house to do hospice care in the living room there. I spent seven days lying by her side. I'd been in Houston for almost two weeks when she woke up and was fully herself, looking at me like she knew who I was. We had a good five minutes while she was alert. It wasn't much time, but it was everything to me. I didn't have that with my brother or my father. It was a gift to be able to have that final conversation with her. I got to tell her that she was the best mother I could imagine. I got to tell her goodbye. And I got to hear her final wishes.

"Don't ever leave your brothers," she said to me. "Don't forget them. Don't fight with them." She had been the center of our family, the mediator, the heart, and now she was asking me to step into that role. Tony was the caregiver. Tosin was the entertainer. She wanted me to be the glue.

When she passed, Tony wasn't home, but Tosin and I were by her side. The nurse told us it was the end. We held her hands. She woke up, briefly, and looked at us. We were trying to be brave, but Tosin was crying, and I was squeezing him under the table. I didn't want his grief to be the last thing she saw. I saw her take a breath. I saw her release the breath. Just as she did, Tony walked in the house. I saw her eyes change. I saw her go.

Tony said, "Wake up, wake up. No. Wake up."

Just then, I remembered something Tosin had told me when Tope died. He'd seen one of my aunts hitting the bed where he was lying after he passed, telling him to stop joking. Tony was doing the same thing now. We'd known for days that this was the end, but it was still difficult to accept that there was no miracle coming in the final hour.

After the coroner came, a few family members showed up, along with Kim and Kristy's mom and dad. I sat on the stairs and cried. When I lost Tope and my father, I had wept behind closed doors, but this time I didn't have to wear any armor. I didn't have to be strong for anyone, not even my mother. Half of my family was dead. I was free to grieve. And so I cried like a baby.

The funeral was planned to be an open casket, so the funeral parlor offered us an employee to do her makeup. I insisted on doing it myself. Everyone tried to talk me out of it, but how could I not? My mother loved it when I did her makeup. It was last thing I could do for her. Max and Kristy came with me. I put a red lipstick on her—she always wore red lipstick. And I did her nails—they were always red and always done and I knew she'd be happy to have them looking fresh at her farewell. She used to always beg me to put eyelashes on her, and I'd tell her she didn't need them. Now, I knew she would have wanted them, so I put them on her. I put her in her best jewelry and sprayed her with White Diamond, her signature scent.

Speak

Growing up, I used to love to lay my head gently on her chest, just to smell her. At the funeral, when I went up to say goodbye, I started to rest my head one more time on her chest. Everyone tried to pull me off her (you're definitely not supposed to reach in a casket at a funeral for all sorts of health and other reasons), but I fought them off. It was like when my mother had sat in my brother's car, wanting to feel connected, wanting to do anything to feel the person again. When I lost my brother, all of my energy and grief went toward helping my parents. When I lost my father, I knew I had survived before and could find the strength to get through it. But when I lost my mom, I lost my best friend. It was like nothing I'd ever experienced.

This time in my speech to our friends and family, I told them how I am who I am because of my mother. I was at her hip for so many years. I had watched her do the same with my niece—they cooked together in the kitchen. They went to garage sales together. They painted their nails and made jewelry together. It was like I was seeing my childhood again, seeing my mother pass on the same legacy, teaching her how to boil the perfect white rice, building her character through her gentle steadiness. I always tell my brothers they're lucky they had kids young, because I would have liked to see my parents with my children. I can picture it, easily, but I still would have liked to see it. She was proud and humble and generous. I think my words did her justice.

She had left her three surviving children: me, Tony, and Tosin; and four grandchildren. No matter how strong our memories, these are the holes that our loved ones leave. When I first lost my mother, I kept picking up my phone and starting to call her before I remembered she was gone. Then, I'd listen to old voicemails that I'd saved just to hear her. When I'm sick, there's nobody I want to call but my mother. When I have wins or moments to celebrate, I know what my parents would say, probably word for word, but just knowing what they would say doesn't make up for them not being here to say it themselves.

I took her wishes to keep the family together to heart. I make a point of going to see my brothers, nephews, and niece every Thanksgiving and Christmas, and honored her instructions not to fight with Tosin. We had been the closest as kids, but always bickered over little things. If I was cooking, he'd say it needed more salt. Or it was dry. Or he'd stand over my shoulder and ask why I was putting grains in everything. Tosin is the most emotional of us, but he hides his sensitivity, partly by trying to get a rise out of people. It has nothing to do with me, I've learned, and everything about him needing to be the center of attention, but it still would get under my skin. My mom told me I was never going to change who he was, so I needed to stop getting upset. One of the last Thanksgivings we had as a family, we'd argued, and she had said, "You guys are getting too old to be doing this. When are you going to learn to just get along?"

There's nobody who makes my blood boil more than Tosin Oyeneyin, but I have not fought with him in the more than ten years since my mother died. He still picks fights with me, but I say to myself, *I'm not going to fight with this boy*, and I try not to engage. When you lose someone, it can bring you together, but when it's the person who was the center of the family, there's a danger that it will distance you. I know how important it was to her that the family still be a family.

Before I'd gone home to LA, I'd done as much as I could to get the house in order. While cleaning out her closet, I found gifts that she had already bought for Kim's unborn daughter—in the hospital, when Mom had seen Kim's belly, she'd made her lift her dress so she could touch the baby. (Kim kept the clothes. I like to think that one day when I have a daughter she'll get to wear the clothes that her grandmother picked out.)

When you lose someone, people tell you that one day you'll be okay again, that you'll redefine yourself around the absence of your loved one. After I lost my mom, three years after my dad and six years after my brother, I knew I needed to allow myself time to grieve. I took two months off work. People checked in on me, but I didn't want to respond. I was unapologetic about taking the time I needed. I was down. I wasn't myself. I wasn't the same friend or colleague. Losing my parents brought with it two interwoven reactions. First, I wondered who I belonged to. Who would be proud of me? Who was I working to please? Who would celebrate my accomplishments with me? Then, I felt a release from responsibility—a kind of freedom. If I messed up, there was nobody to let down. I didn't have to fear disappointing them. And I didn't have to worry about their well-being anymore. There was nobody watching me. After all this tragedy, I could coast. If I was a bad friend, my friends would understand. If I didn't show up at work, people would understand.

Grieving had changed me each time, and each time it led me exactly where I needed to be. I started seeing a therapist. I journaled. I found my way through. The worst thing imaginable had happened to me. Again. But I was still lucky. I had had an incredible mother for twenty-nine years. For twenty-nine years, she reminded me who I was, and whose daughter I was. She always said, "Look at you, Black and shine." When I was growing up, I thought she was talking about my shiny skin, but now I understand what she was talking about. She wanted me to use my voice. She taught me how, not by saying "Speak up and use your voice," but by example. She knew how to get her message across, even when the person she was talking to had opposing views. She got through to both sides. I continue to build on her legacy every day. Everything I do, I do for her.

Eventually, I realized that I hadn't only been the good girl for my parents. In the end, the person I always had to show up for was myself. When you first learn to ride a bicycle, your parents hold on to the bike and run alongside you as you pedal. And then, at some point, you realize that they've taken their hands away, and you're riding the bike all by yourself. At first you wobble. You thought they were supporting you. You'll fall without them! But no, you've been pedaling this whole time. You can do it.

When my parents left, I looked down and realized I knew how to balance. I was already moving ahead. They had been cheering from the sidelines for a while already.

There came a day some time ago when I made the decision to believe in myself. Life changes gears in an instant. Sometimes the chain catches, but if you keep pushing, things shift into place, and you lock into the new rhythm. You begin to adapt to what is in front of you. It wouldn't do my brother, my father, or my mother any good if I gave up on my own joy. I live and move and do because they can't. They've been a clear testament to the fact that life is short, and everything is temporary.

During one of the seminars that I did with the young women who'd been in abusive relationships, I talked to them about the losses I'd gone through. After the meeting was over, some of the girls started to leave, but others lingered. The makeup I'd brought from the office was expensive, so I spent some time explaining how they could replicate what I'd done with drugstore purchases.

Gradually, all the girls left except for one. She was tall, with blond hair and glasses, and was obviously waiting for everyone else to leave to get up the courage to talk to me. I could tell, just from how she dressed and interacted with the others, that she had trouble connecting. Each of these girls had a different, hard story, and I didn't know hers. When it was just us in the room, I asked, "Did you have a good time today?"

"I just wanted to say thank you," she said.

"I'm so happy—I loved being here," I told her. And it was true. This was exactly what I loved to do, whether it was at a makeup counter, in a cycling class, or anywhere else.

She pushed her glasses back. "I thought about ending it all. But after today and hearing your story, I'm gonna give it a second chance."

Her words took my breath away. We hugged and I held her. (And after she left, I told the doctors who ran the program. I was glad to help her, but her needs were clearly beyond my abilities.)

It makes me uncomfortable, sometimes, that my life has made people count their blessings, that my losses are a reminder that they're lucky. But in that moment, my life had served as a model for that girl's pain, and the ability to overcome it. It made me feel like maybe I'd gone through all of this because I was supposed to share my story with people who had similar struggles.

For Mother's Day 2021, I wrote a letter to my mom that was published in *Well+Good*, an online magazine.

Dear Mom,

It's been some time since we've laid eyes on one another. Although I can no longer see you in human form, I know that our souls are more connected now than ever before. A lot has changed since you left. We've all grown, started new careers, ended them, and started new again. I wish you were still here to share in my joy and to celebrate my wins as your own. Sometimes when I think of you, I dream of having a chance to thank you for all of the selfless hours turned days, weeks, and years that you invested in me, my well-being, and my happiness.

What I would give to know you as the world knew you: As just Veronica and not "Mom," "Mommy," or "MOM!" I'm old enough now to fully appreciate you for all that you were. I find myself daydreaming about what it would have been like to have been your colleague or friend. I imagine I would have admired you for your work ethic and the love and care that you provided to your patients. If I was your friend, I would have valued your ability to listen and support, and I'm sure I would have enjoyed trading clothes from your infamous walk-in closet.

So much has changed and yet so much has remained the same. The values you instilled in us remain the same. I've grown into the woman you always saw me as, even though I didn't quite see her in myself. You taught me how to hold space and make my presence felt in a room. You showed me that my mind was my most powerful asset and my strongest muscle. You told me that the best way to change was to make changes. You enabled me to see that, while the world flocked towards you for your beauty, it was your words that kept their attention. You taught me not to doubt uncertainty. You reminded me that uncertainty would lead me to a land of infinite and unimaginable possibility. You showed me that I would hold the key to my own success, that ultimately, anything that I wanted out of life was already mine if I was willing to see it for myself and work hard to obtain it.

Twenty-nine years is a long time to own a pair of heels or an antique dresser, but twenty-nine years with you wasn't enough. When I sit in silence and quiet the thoughts in my head, I look to the sky at night and I see your face. I listen as the wind rustles between the leaves and reflect on the lessons you taught me, acknowledging the person I've become because of you.

Today, I searched for a picture that captured the energy you brought to this world. I wanted a photo that encompassed some of your most defining traits. I looked for one that showed your sarcasm, your wit, your power, and your grace. I searched for a picture that would perfectly display our mother-daughter connection and your grand love for your children. I wanted to find something that embodied who you are with one single glance. I searched and I searched and then I stopped looking. When I look for you, I find me. I am you—I am all of you. You helped craft me into the woman I am. The person that I show up as every day is a result of the love and trust that you poured into me: I am smart, I am kind, and I am beautiful. I am a leader and a listener. I am courageous, bold, and although I sometimes waiver, I always come back to being so unapologetically me. I have a sharp mouth and always stand up, speak up, and rise up to all that I believe is true. I am me, but I am also you.

I feel you in my spirit perhaps more than I did when you were here in living form. My sense of humor, my power, my humility, my ability to love—all that I am, I am because of you.

Speak

Mommy, if you are able to receive letters in heaven I just want you to know that we love you and we miss you from here down below.

I love you too much,
Yetunde

Originally published by *Well+Good* in March 2021.

TWELVE

Life Cycles

Life is kind of like a cycling class. When you first start moving, no matter how little resistance you're facing, it's tough to get started. You need to adjust yourself to the bike. You need to get used to the motions. You need to get a feel for the road. And then, just when you're warming up and think you can handle it, you hit a hill. It's steep and it's hard. You're not sure you can make it. You slow down when you have to, rise out of your seat to reallocate your energy. But if you keep moving forward, you'll make it to the top. And when you reach a peak, things will get easier for a bit. It's flat. You recover. You breathe deeply, take a sip of water. You feel a bit of pride. You're not done, but you just made it up that hill, and if you could do that, who knows what else you can accomplish? And then—out of nowhere—come intervals. Those short, torturous spurts of intensity that drive you to exhaustion, but give you just enough time in between to catch your breath and ride the next wave. And just when you think you can't go any farther? You're blessed with another recovery right before you head back into an extended climb. It takes whatever you've got left. But you always finish victorious.

How do we deal with this ride we're on? The ups, the downs, the unexpected turns, the sweat, the tears, the Wi-Fi outages that bring everything to a crashing halt.

My advice? Drink a lot of water. (That's not a metaphor. Water's really good for you.)

I had only been working at Peloton for seven months when the COVID-19 pandemic hit. At first, like most businesses and gyms, the studio shut down completely. I didn't know very many people in New York, so when that happened, it was hard to stay disciplined. I was eating junk food. I couldn't drag myself up to exercise. It was hard to even make it to the shower. News stories said that deodorant sales dropped, and ice cream sales skyrocketed. (I was definitely one of the people contributing to that trend. Nobody could smell me over Zoom.) I felt disappointed in myself for my lack of motivation until Jess Sims said to me, "Tunde, have you ever been in a pandemic before?"

I told her I hadn't.

"Then why are you being so hard on yourself? You can't measure pandemic Tunde against pre-pandemic Tunde."

When the batteries in our phones drop to ten percent, we panic. We scramble to find an outlet so that we can charge it before it goes completely dead. But we let ourselves run down to ten all the time. We wait until the last possible second, when we see the shutdown most imminently, to find a solution. What if we had the same urgency when it came to taking care of ourselves? And what if we felt it before our own batteries get dangerously low?

People think of self-care—like getting our hair or nails done—as a luxury. Though I love doing that just as much as anyone, I prefer to think of things as "soul-care." A meditation. A walk. A bath. A facial. All of these things help us on the outside but give us much more on the inside. I think of mothers who are judged for taking time out of their days to work out. People will say she's being selfish, or vain. But that thirty-minute investment in herself does more than help her sweat or burn some calories or tone her abs—it allows her the space to show up for herself, which ultimately helps her to show up and be the best partner, wife, mother, friend. We have to be good to ourselves so that we can show up for everyone else.

When the pandemic hit, even more people turned to Peloton to work out, so once public health regulations allowed it, we went back to teaching—alone—in the studio. The amount of people in a live class quadrupled, but I couldn't see them. Imagine Coldplay performing a concert to an empty stadium. Every day I was going on stage to perform, but I felt disconnected from myself. I couldn't hear the drumbeat. *Could riders tell?* I worried as I started and finished each ride. I don't know, but I realized the opportunity I had, to use what I was feeling to relate to them and find out. I told them everything I was telling myself. I tried to help them find their motivation using the same words that helped me find mine. It was the ultimate form of soul-care.

And, slowly, it worked. I started small, believing that any and every accomplishment was a win. Using deodorant again: win. Brushing and flossing my teeth: win. Leaving the apartment: win. The little things matter—in fact, they add up to more than the big things. On her last day on earth, I looked into my mother's eyes. I watched her inhale and exhale. Her pupils dilated, and I saw her soul transition. In that moment, I felt so connected to her. It was like I could feel and hear her without speaking. What I felt radiating from her soul wasn't the so-called big wins—the promotions, the game shows, the cars—but the little ones, like my first birthday party, her braiding my hair with me on the floor between her legs. The last laugh we shared together. My brother's children climbing all over her as they watched a movie.

New York was the epicenter of the pandemic, and I'd been so afraid to be around people that I'd cut the length of my dog's walks in half, never stopping to sit on a bench or let him play. After a while, I started to work to regain my confidence. I started taking Cesar out on longer walks. I was still careful, masked, but before long I was picking up coffee and exchanging hellos with people again.

One sunny, beautiful day in the middle of our walk,

Cesar jumped up on a bench to take in the sun. "Come on, Cesar, we need to get back inside," I told him, tugging gently at his leash. But his wild, beautiful soul was intent on keeping me in the present moment. He sat on the bench and his eyes told me to do the same. So, I sat there next to him and let the sun hit my skin. My shoulders dropped. The heaviness of the world dropped. For months we had been trapped on an island in the middle of an apocalyptic movie, and this felt like the first time I had stopped to breathe. I felt the warmth of the day, and I was so grateful for Cesar. He looked at me like he knew exactly what I needed in that moment. From there I slowly started to get back into my routine. From that came discipline. The drumbeat led me back to the surface.

The pandemic had slowed everything down. I was alone, and the isolation of quarantine highlighted that. At almost thirty-six years old, I was single. When I was in my twenties, I had had an idea that Prince Charming would appear before me. I wanted to "get chose" by a man. My friend Jessica used to joke about it every time she saw me. She'd ask, "You still trying to get chose?"

I was so far from that mindset now. I wasn't looking for a man to choose me anymore. I was the one doing the choosing.

Growing up with a full house, I lived with people constantly running up and down the stairs. Everyone made "yo mama" jokes even though we all had the same mother. I had always assumed I would have a big, chaotic family of my own one day, because I had grown up in one. I had never understood why some people didn't want to have kids—I didn't judge it, but it was hard for me to relate to that choice. Then, my brothers had children. My friends had children. I saw how much work it was and started to think that maybe I didn't need *so* many children.

I thought I needed love to plan for a child, but I was warming up to making big decisions on my own. My parents were gone. The training wheels were off. I'd been riding by myself for a while, and I was willing and ready to take action. Whenever we make big decisions, it's easier if there's someone else there, affirming our choices, deciding alongside us, or taking the lead. But ultimately, even the decisions we make with a partner are ours. We own them. Big decisions don't get in the way of love. The stillness allowed me to realize that I didn't have a family because I hadn't put my attention on building one—and that was okay. It hadn't come for me because I hadn't put thought into it. But as I got older, that mindset came into focus. I still wanted to be a mom, but I no longer felt like it was an absolute certainty. To parent is to serve, and there are many ways of serving. I could foster; I could adopt. I could work with children. I could work with organizations that help children. I could serve in some completely different way.

I decided that when the time came that I wanted to have children, I wanted to maximize my chances of being able to get pregnant. I trusted that a family would happen for me, in one way or another, so I decided to keep my options open by freezing my eggs. Science could give me the freedom to let love happen naturally. I was open to love and to the next chapter. I could wait for it to happen. I was fortunate enough to be able to make a decision based on the direction my life was taking, instead of being constrained by what I thought the direction had to be.

They say that some people are in your life for a season and some for a reason. Brian, my first serious boyfriend, obviously hadn't worked out, but I didn't regret that relationship. I learned so much from him. After that breakup, I went on a lot of dates. I was swiping left, right, up, and down, sometimes even going on two dates a night. Some of them were terrible. But after each one I'd ask myself, *What did you learn from this date?* I learned I'm not a fan of guys who want me to pick up the check on the first date. I'm turned off by guys who talk about their ex-girlfriend the whole night. I definitely don't like men who take business calls throughout a show. If the universe pushed someone in front of me, no matter the outcome, there was a reason. It helped me feel more sure that when I met the right person, it would be because I'd put together everything I'd learned.

I had a boyfriend when I got the job at Peloton. Johnny is a good man, but at the time he didn't respect cycling—he joked that it was just a bike that went nowhere. He couldn't believe I was taking the job, and I couldn't believe he didn't respect that I was taking such a huge opportunity. When we discussed whether he should come to New York with me, I didn't want him to leave his dream to watch me chase mine, and have it be held over my head. I didn't want to get in a fight about toilet paper and then have him bring up that he had moved across the country for me.

Robin once said to me that she'd married herself before she married her husband. So, I started dating myself. In isolation, I tried out new hobbies to discover what fulfilled me. I worked a lot and decided that I could be selfish about my time and energy—all the things that you don't always get to do fully when there are other people to consider. You're never done growing, but I think that before you are really ready to love someone else, you should be established in your views and beliefs. You should know who you are, what you want, what you like, and what you don't like. That way, when you do find someone, you'll have your full self to give because you've accepted yourself and understand yourself fully.

Now and then, I watch kids blowing bubbles in Central Park. They make the biggest bubbles they can, perfectly round, floating up into the air. Sometimes the bubbles touch, but don't connect. And sometimes they connect. When they do, occasionally two bubbles form one bigger bubble. That's not what I'm looking for. I don't want to merge into another person. But sometimes two bubbles attach, and there's a flat part where they latch on, while still maintaining their original shape. That's what I want. I'm not looking to complete myself with another person. I'm looking to extend myself. I'm looking for someone to expand with. I'm a sphere. They're a sphere. We'll travel along beside each other. One night, I saw a young couple sitting on the steps of a building. She was leaning her head against him. Such a small gesture, but when you're single, you see how much it adds to life to have that shoulder and to be that shoulder. Love is a such a huge part of life. I'm not in a rush to fall in love just for the sake of being in love, but I'm ready to complete my bubble so that I can bump into someone else's and grow with them. I know much more about myself than I did ten years ago. I respect myself so much more. I can understand people and their needs more. I'm a better giver and a better listener. Because of where I am, the people I allow into my circle, whether in a romantic relationship or a friendship, will respect me, understand me, and give to me, too. I am treating myself better, so I know how I deserve to be treated.

I'd gotten through a pandemic alone, turned thirty-five, shaved my hair off, and frozen my eggs. I'd come a long way from Katy, where my brothers and cousins and parents and I made a loud, warm home in the blue house with brick sides and a red door. For a long time, I'd put off the idea of buying a home until I met the person I wanted to raise children and spend the rest of my life with. But I was done waiting for life to happen. It was summer, soon to be fall, and I wanted to be fully alive in every season of my life. I wanted a neighborhood. I started looking for a place to call home.

One day, after looking for five months, I saw a beautiful condo in Brooklyn. It had high ceilings. The bathroom was an oasis. There were plenty of trees in the neighborhood and a park nearby. Cesar would love that. I could walk there. Maybe with a man. Maybe with a baby. Maybe with another dog. Love is in my future, I know that.

As I was leaving the house, I thought of my parents and hoped that they'd send me a sign. Then I turned to look back at the building. It was then I realized that, just like the house I'd grown up in, it was brick with blue gates and a red door. A week later my offer was accepted.

When you invest deep love in anyone, you risk great heartbreak. I watched my mother suffer at losing her child and couldn't think of anything harder. When I hold Cesar, who is thirteen years old, I can't imagine my life without this dog. It seems unbearable. And yet, that day will come. We can't let fear of what isn't disrupt what already is. Because with the risk of heartbreak is the greatest reward. New York holds every truth in its palm, and not long after I saw that young couple on the stoop, embodying the simplicity of love, I saw a Black man with his son. The street was closed off for construction, so the two of them were the only people standing at the end of it, and they were having a real man-to-man talk. Maybe the boy was going off to college. It looked like they were saying goodbye, and it was full of love and pain and life, as if the father had done as much as he could to prepare him for the joys and protect him from the dangers of the world, and now he was letting him go. There was such beauty, even in heartbreak, because of how much the love mattered. So much of the pain I've experienced in my life has been tied to love. To love is to accept pain, to take it in, to grow from it, and to love again.

Afterword

Life matters. We matter. Each of us in all our imperfection. The jobs we hate. The breakups. The missed opportunities. The doubt. The worry. The losses. All the subconscious messiness we carry around with us. All the pain is part of the joy. I know this from cycling. I know it from life. I feel it every day. We matter alone in our homes, where we push to change ourselves and our lives, when we fight for everything we hold dear. We matter together, as we connect, learn, diverge, and pull each other close. We're different. We're the same. We know this in our hearts. We feel our power as we step forward into our true selves. We recognize and understand each other, even through our differences.

When I talk about love, I think about my bubble connecting with someone else's, but what I really want is for all of our bubbles to touch and connect. I want us to see each other as we are and to celebrate each other for who we are and all we have to give. I love living in my skin, and I am deeply inspired by others who live boldly in theirs. My friends, family, teammates, the people I meet on the subway and in my day-to-day interactions who show up as themselves, in all their bold glory. I'm inspired by the brave people whose lives touch mine without us ever meeting. I'm moved by the lyrics to a song, a great podcast, or even a new favorite book. These are the winds that breathe oxygen as we spark the flame to ignite our own fires. They say the sky's the limit, but even the sky is too close. Because you see it. Where do I see my momentum taking me next? I don't know, but I surrender to where the drum leads me.

From a very young age, my mother always used to say, "Black and shine. Black and shine. Black and shine. Wow." She would look at me in amazement. What she saw in me, I can now see in myself. The power she recognized, I feel in myself. This was her gift to me, a gift that she was always trying to give me, but I wasn't receiving. She left it here for me to unwrap. By the time I was able to open it up and see what was inside, she was gone. But the gift that she gave me of recognizing my power will last forever.

This is the season to step into your own.

This is the season to acknowledge your value, your uniqueness.

This is the season to see yourself fully for who you are.

Be your own inspiration, and then spark the light for others.

Find your voice, trust your gut, and SPEAK, because we're all listening.

Acknowledgments

The drumbeat I follow, the hum of it. The sound the waves make when they crash in the deep blue ocean— these are my connection to the Universe, to Source, to God. I thank you.

In life and in book writing, we are never alone. I am able to SPEAK because of the people around me, and I am so grateful to them.

My first dream as a child was to one day write a book and share my story, a story that didn't yet exist. To Ben Loehnen, Meredith Vilarello, Julianna Haubner, Jofie Ferrari-Adler, and the entire team at Avid Reader Press, thank you for your hand in making that dream a reality.

To my literary agent Kari Stuart, who helped me convince the publisher I'd have this book done in time. I'm forever grateful. To Hilary Liftin, with whom I wrote this book—can you believe we actually did get it done on time?!

Acknowledgments

You were able to piece together my thoughts when I couldn't see the whole puzzle. To my agents Katie Baral, Jen Rudin, Lindsay Samakow, Justin Ongert, and Chris Sawtelle. The drum beats and you're able to recognize its vibration. Thank you for fighting for spaces where it can be heard. To my manager Kim Harvey . . . yep same Kim. Friend—sister—manager. Outside of our friendship, I have to first acknowledge you for the day-to-day role you play in my life. This was supposed to be a temporary thing until I figured out the next step. And here we are still stepping at it together. It's an absolute joy to watch you move into your full power. I'm so proud of us. To Adele Oliver, thank you for the time you give me back on a daily basis. The time that gave me the space to tell this story.

To my sister friends Kim Harvey and Kristy Caldwell—I did it! I finally wrote the book! So much of my story is "our" story. We were put here to find each other, and I'd choose you to do life with every time. Thank you for being flames that spark the light in my life. Thank you for being my people. To Callye Peyrovi and JoAnn Bogwu, who have always been my biggest advocates, you fight for me even when I don't need fighting for. To Billie Ferguson, you always remind me when it's time to adjust my crown and, just as important, when it's sitting upright and perfectly straight. To Jessica Khan and Erika Guinn, you showed me what it was to own the power of your voices. To Erica Siciliano and Nikki Key Playter, you always find the perfect words. To Jade Smith and Latosha Lovell, you never let me forget what I bring to the table.

Acknowledgments

To Max Bronner, I have more than a hundred saved memos from the late nights I've spent talking to you on the phone over the years. Our spiritual awakenings arrived at the exact same moment. It was many of those late-night chats that led me here. I'm so grateful LA gave me you. To Johnny D' Esposito, we grew up a lot together, didn't we? You will forever be in my heart.

To Mimi Benz, thank for giving me my first job in fitness. You saw my power when I didn't. To Cody Rigsby, who dropped a line in my DMs and changed my life. I love you, boo. To Jen Cotter, Kevin Chorlins, Robin Arzón, Randy Roth, for my second chance; and to all of my Peloton team, on-screen and off-, those of you who had a voice in my arrival, those of you who on a daily basis inspire me to redefine what I think my best is. To the Peloton community, although we interface through a touchscreen, your support has provided me with the opportunity to live out my wildest dreams and to share this story. I'm grateful to be a part of your journey and I'm blessed to have you here as a part of mine.

To my aunties, uncles, and cousins who showered us with love in our darkest hours. Sometimes when I wake in the middle of the night, I look around wondering who the hell's house I'm in, questioning why I'm not fourteen. I'm not sure if that's because time really does fly or because a part of me still holds on to the way I remember us as kids, before the loss and the heartache that I speak to in this book. To my oldest brother, Toyin, whom I spell as T-o-n-y in the book only because that's how he'd prefer it. Thank you for stepping in to play the role of both father and mother in my life. To my second brother, Tosin . . . Ha! Shocked you're being acknowledged? Yeah, me too. You are all fun and games on the outside, but I know your heart is pure and fragile. Thank you for always playing the role of protector. When I realize I'm in my bed under the sheets that I paid for and that all the trauma we've seen really did happen—I'm happy that we aren't frozen in place and that time has in fact moved on because it brought me the loves of my life.

To my babies!!! My brother's kids Tayo, (whom I refer to as Silas in this book again because he'd prefer it that way), entrepreneur at the age of nineteen, your willingness to dream is a gift. Don't ever lose that. And Temi, my sweet love, Black and shine. You are wise beyond your years, baby girl. And T.J., your thoughtfulness and the way you love is your superpower. Don't tell your daddy, but you get it from him. Tony, future President of the World—that's not actually a thing yet, but if there is one day, I'd put my bet on you. Your mind is fascinating. I can't wait to see where you take it. To my extended family, you know who you are. You have always showed up.

Mama C., Ivan, Grams—you've always made me feel like part of the family. I AM family. To my brother-in-law Jordan Harvey, thank you for being the example of what it is to be a partner.

To Harlow, Nate, Bear, and Houston—I love you the way that I love my own.

And finally, to the most unconditional love I know, my Cesar boy. Thank you for making my life richer.

About the Author

Tunde Oyeneyin, a Texas native of Nigerian descent, is a motivational speaker and a Peloton instructor, training nearly 20,000 riders on any given day. She began her career as a professional makeup artist and brand educator for some of the most sought-after beauty lines in the world. She was named a face of Revlon cosmetics and a Nike athlete in 2021. Tunde has been featured on *Today* and *Good Morning America*, in the *New York Times*, *Vanity Fair*, *Vogue*, and more. She lives in Brooklyn, New York, with her dog, Cesar. This is her first book.

To find Tunde, please visit:
www.speaktunde.com
IG: @tune2tunde
TikTok: @tune2tunde